Bill Bernbach's Book

A History of the Advertising That Changed the History of Advertising

 Villard Books New York 1987

Bill
Bernbach's
Book

by Bob Levenson

Copyright © 1987 by Evelyn Bernbach and Bob Levenson
All rights reserved under International and Pan-American
Copyright Conventions. Published in the United States by
Villard Books, a division of Random House, Inc., New York,
and simultaneously in Canada by Random House of
Canada Limited, Toronto.

Grateful acknowledgment is made to *Harper's* magazine
for permission to reprint an excerpt from ''Obituary,
William Bernbach'' by Michael Kingsley. Copyright © 1983
by *Harper's* magazine. All rights reserved. Reprinted from
the March 1983 issue by special permission.

''You Don't Have to Be Jewish to Love Levy's Real Jewish
Rye,'' copyright © 1970 Arnold Foods Company, Inc.

Rheingold's ad reproduced courtesy of C. Schmidt & Sons,
Incorporated, D/B/A Rheingold Brewery.

Ohrbach's ads reproduced courtesy of Ohrbach's, Inc.

Chivas Regal ads used by permission of General Wine &
Spirits Co. Copyright General Wine & Spirits Co., New
York, N.Y. Chivas and Chivas Regal are registered
trademarks of Chivas Brothers Limited.

Bally print ad used by permission of Bally Arola Ag.

Calvert ad used by permission of Joseph E. Seagram &
Sons, Inc. Copyright © 1963 by Calvert Distillers, Co.
Calvert and Calvert Extra are registered trademarks of
Joseph E. Seagram & Sons, Inc.

Library of Congress Cataloging-in-Publication Data
Levenson, Bob.
Bill Bernbach's book.
1. Advertising—United States—History.
2. Bernbach, Bill.
II. Title.
HF5813.U6L48 1987   659.1'0973   86-40103
ISBN 0-394-54920-1

Manufactured in Italy by Sagdos S.p.A.,
Brugherio (Milano)
9 8 7 6 5 4 3 2
First Edition
Book design: Elissa Ichiyasu

For Evelyn, John and Paul Bernbach,
who asked me to.

Above all for Kathe,
who forced me to.

We know for certain that Bill wrote the dedication expressly for this book.

But we know little else about the book; it was his secret project.

We don't know exactly what he wanted it to look like or exactly how he wanted it to sound.

We do know that he wanted it.

To that end, Evelyn Bernbach, his widow, and his sons, John and Paul, asked me to try to put Bill's book together, to give it a look and a voice, and, above all, to coax it into being in his spirit.

I have worked with his work itself, with his speeches, with countless interviews and articles by him and about him, and with a number of taped transcripts in which he outlined many of his thoughts.

I knew Bill. I believe that I knew him well. I worked for him and with him for nearly a quarter of a century. We shared many good times and many good thoughts and more than a few nasty problems.

But a predictable man he was not. Nor had he ever written a book. Nor had I.

So what this has turned out to be is a book by one man about what another man's book might have been if either of them had ever written a book before.

He would have loved the irony and the challenge. I can only hope that he would have loved the result.

Bob Levenson

Dedication

This book is a thank-you note to the many who have carried me in their talented hands over the long journey of my life and work.

I thank the great DDB art directors and copywriters, wherever they are, for breathing beautiful life into my communications philosophy. They were not at all like P. G. Wodehouse's young daughter, to whom he offered this dedication in one of his books: "To my daughter without whose help this book would have been finished in half the time." My work would indeed never have been finished without the great talents of Bob Gage, Phyllis Robinson, Bob Levenson, Helmut Krone, and so many others; without the business wisdom and moral support of Mac Dane, Ned Doyle, and Joe Daly.

When we started our agency, we had in mind precisely the kind of people we wanted with us. There were two requirements: You had to be talented and you had to be nice. If you were nice but without talent, we were very sorry but you just wouldn't do. We had to "make it," and only great talent would help us do that. If you were a great talent but not a nice person, we had no hesitation in saying "No." Life is too short to sacrifice so much of it to living with a bastard. It's a wonderful feeling to know that we built an organization where nice guys didn't finish last.

I thank our clients who had the courage (and the money) to help us break new ground. More and more I have come to the conclusion that a principle isn't a principle until it costs you money. Our clients believed with us that the most important ingredient in the success of an advertising campaign is the product itself. They believed with us that you say something better when you have something to say. And they understood that advertising doesn't create a better product. It only conveys it. They believed with us that good art, good writing, and good taste can be good advertising.

I will never forget the client who, outraged by the false claims of his competitor, said, "Bill, we'll show him. I've got a great gimmick. Let's tell the truth." Nor will I soon forget the client who, addressing his employees, said, "We are in a service business and I know it *pays* to be courteous but I urge you to be courteous for another reason. It is so much a better way to live. It is a difficult life at best and thoughtfulness can multiply the pleasant moments." Kenneth Clark, the eminent art critic, was later to express the same thought when he wrote in his great book *Civilization,* "I believe in courtesy, the ritual by which we avoid hurting other people's feelings by satisfying our own egos. And I think we should remember that we are part of a great whole, which for convenience we call nature. All living things are our brothers and sisters."

And I thank these clients for knowing instinctively that for creative people rules can be prisons.

Yes, rules can get you in trouble.

I thank our clients for believing so deeply in truth in advertising.

And I thank them for understanding that in this case, virtue isn't its own reward. They knew that as far as advertising budgets are concerned, the truth isn't the truth until people believe you; and they can't believe you if they don't know what you're saying; and they can't know what you're saying if they don't listen to you; and they won't listen to you if you're not interesting. And you won't be interesting unless you say things freshly, originally, imaginatively.

I thank them for knowing that knowledge is the *beginning,* not the end, of effectiveness; that knowledge is ultimately available to everyone; and that the only thing that's yours and yours alone is a great idea, memorably expressed. No one can ever take that from you.

Finally, I want to thank my family and friends. A man finds it difficult to express his deeply felt sentiments in private. It is so much easier in public. Well, at last I have the occasion. I thank my wife and my sons and my very close friends for an indulgence that could only be born out of love, for listening to me endlessly over the years on my favorite subject of communications and showing no signs of the boredom they had every right to feel, and for just being around when I needed them. They're wonderful, and I want to put it on the record.

We in the communications field—in radio, in television, in magazines, in newspapers, in posters—have developed unprecedented skills in mass persuasion. You and I can no longer isolate our lives. It just won't work. What happens to society is going to affect us with ever-increasing rapidity. The world has progressed to the point where its most powerful force is public opinion. And I believe that in this new, complex, dynamic world it is not the great book or the epic play, as once was the case, that will shape that opinion, but those who understand mass media and the techniques of mass persuasion. The metabolism of the world has changed. New vehicles must carry ideas to it. We must ally ourselves with great ideas and carry them to the public. We must practice our skills in behalf of society. We must not just believe in what we sell. We must sell what we believe in. And we must pour a vast energy into these causes.

Above all, this book is dedicated to those who will continue to energetically pursue this kind of vision, who will make the great contributions to our world of communications in the days and years ahead.

Bill Bernbach

Acknowledg-ments

Luckily, I didn't have to do this book without the cheerful, willing help of Gigi Glassman, Melissa London, Elsa Beste and, especially, Charlie Abrams.

My good friend Nancy Underwood, who was Bill's secretary and confidante for more than twenty years, provided materials I never knew existed, and invaluable guidance from her unique vantage point.

Teresa McVeigh, who has been at my side for long years, did what she always does: save me from myself with affection I don't deserve and with wisdom far greater than my own.

The greatest tribute is for those who embraced the idea, who made the point, who did the work: the good people of Doyle Dane Bernbach.

Contents

Dedication / ix

Acknowledgments / xi

Introduction / xv

Ohrbach's / 2

Levy's / 10

El Al Israel Airlines / 18

Volkswagen / 26

Avis / 52

Mobil / 60

Chivas Regal / 68

Polaroid / 78

American Airlines / 88

Clairol / 98

Colombian Coffee / 104

Porsche / 110

Alka-Seltzer / 118

Utica Club, Rheingold, Stroh's / 122

Jamaica / 130

Life Cereal / 138

Sara Lee / 142

O. M. Scott / 146

Why This Book Isn't on Wheels / 153

Another Bill Bernbach / 193

Other People, Other Places / 199

Introduction: A Bit of Biography

William Bernbach was born in The Bronx, New York, on August 13, 1911, to Rebecca and Jacob Bernbach.

His father was, in Bill's words, an "austere but elegant" designer of women's clothing.

Bill jokingly maintained that he had no middle name because "his family was too poor," but that wasn't the case. He didn't have to help support his family, as many youngsters did in those days. Instead, he attended New York City public schools and, in 1932, earned a B.A. degree from New York University rather than from tuition-free City College.

He was, therefore, in many ways advantaged.

He saw the Depression and lived through it, but he was not part of it, nor was he hurt by it.

He had a college education, during which he majored in English, but also studied music, business administration, and philosophy. He played the piano. He was born under the sign of Leo. He was bright, observant, articulate, and could reasonably feel that he was a cut above many of the people around him.

On the other hand, he was slight, pale, unathletic, and physically altogether unprepossessing. And, in 1932, this frail, five-foot-seven-inch, blond, blue-eyed, quick-witted package of ego, ambition, confidence, determination, and energy found himself employed by the Schenley Distillers Company as an office boy in the mailroom.

But not for long.

In addition to delivering mail and reading the poetry of Kahlil Gibran, he wrote an ad for Schenley's American Cream Whiskey and made sure that it got to Schenley's advertising department. (Easy enough if you're the one who delivers the mail.)

The ad appeared sometime later, exactly as he had written it, but with no credit to him or for him. By this stage, Bill had made the acquaintance of Mr. Lewis Rosenstiel's (the president of Schenley) secretary and a fellow admirer of Kahlil Gibran. Bill saw to it, through the secretary, that Mr. Rosenstiel found out who the ad's author was. In response, Rosenstiel ordered that Bernbach be given a raise and a job in the advertising department.

The moving hand, having writ, moves on.

In 1939 Bill left Schenley to work as a ghostwriter for Grover Whalen, who was the head of the 1939 World's Fair, which was held in New York.

After the fair, Bill was hired by the William H. Weintraub agency, where he worked with Paul Rand, a graphic and industrial designer whose strength and bold simplicity on the printed page were a powerful influence on Bernbach. Both the friendship and the influence were to last for many years.

After his service in the U.S. Army and a brief job with Coty, Incorporated, Bill joined Grey Advertising as a copywriter. In a matter of months, he became copy chief and soon after became vice-president and creative director.

Bill's remarkably quick rise to the top of the creative department at Grey can be partly accounted for by his unusual verbal, visual, and people skills. But only partly.

He was a visionary, with a visionary's zeal. And he was a worrier. It was a killer combination.

Here, in this altogether revealing letter to the owners of Grey Advertising, we see the fully formed Bill Bernbach. It was written in May 1947, two years before Doyle Dane Bernbach was born. It dealt with issues that were central to him throughout his life and that the majority of the world's agencies have barely begun to recognize or simply pay lip service to, even today.

May 15, 1947

Dear ———:

Our agency is getting big. That's something to be happy about. But it's something to worry about, too, and I don't mind telling you I'm damn worried. I'm worried that we're going to fall into the trap of bigness, that we're going to worship techniques instead of substance, that we're going to follow history instead of making it, that we're going to be drowned by superficialities instead of buoyed up by solid fundamentals. I'm worried lest hardening of the creative arteries begin to set in.

There are a lot of great technicians in advertising. And unfortunately they talk the best game. They know all the rules. They can tell you that people in an ad will get you greater readership. They can tell you that a sentence should be this short or that long. They can tell you that body copy should be broken up for easier and more inviting reading. They can give you fact after fact after fact. They are the scientists of advertising. But there's one little rub. Advertising is fundamentally persuasion and persuasion happens to be not a science, but an art.

It's that creative spark that I'm so jealous of for our agency and that I am so desperately fearful of losing. I don't want academicians. I don't want scientists. I don't want people who do the right things. *I want people who do inspiring things.*

In the past year I must have interviewed about 80 people—writers and artists. Many of them were from the so-called giants of the agency field. It was appalling to see how few of these people were genuinely creative. Sure, they had advertising know-how. Yes, they were up on advertising technique. But look beneath the technique and what did you find? A sameness, a mental weariness, a mediocrity of ideas. But they could defend every ad on the basis that it obeyed the rules of advertising. It was like worshipping a ritual instead of the God.

All this is not to say that technique is unimportant. Superior technical skill will make a good man better. But the danger is a preoccupation with technical skill or the mistaking of technical skill for creative ability. The danger lies in the temptation to buy routinized men who have a formula for advertising. The danger lies in the natural tendency to go after tried-and-true talent that will not make us stand out in competition but rather make us look like all others.

If we are to advance, we must emerge as a distinctive personality. We must develop our own philosophy and not have the advertising philosophy of others imposed on us.

Let us blaze new trails. Let us prove to the world that good taste, good art, good writing can be good selling.

Respectfully,
Bill Bernbach

Apparently, the management at Grey Advertising didn't respond quickly enough for Bill. And in the meantime, he and Ned Doyle, a vice president and account executive at Grey, had formed "a mutuality of respect." (Those are Doyle's words; Bernbach would have said, "We understood each other.") Doyle knew a man called Maxwell Dane who was running a small agency at the time. Mac Dane had a going concern, a good, sound business mind, and was paying the rent for a penthouse on Madison Avenue. ("Penthouse" is a euphemism; actually, the elevator stopped at the top floor, and one had to hike up a long flight of steps to the rooftop office.)

They had almost everything. An outside man (Doyle), an inside man (Dane), a creative man (Bernbach), and office space.

All they lacked was a client and a name.

The client was about to appear. On June 1, 1949, they went into business and named the agency Doyle Dane Bernbach.

"Nothing will ever get between us," Bill said. "Not even punctuation."

The stage was set and nothing ever did.

Bill Bernbach's Book

Ohrbach's

There might not have been a Doyle Dane Bernbach had it not been for the Ohrbach's business. At least not in its current form.

N. M. Ohrbach and Bill Bernbach knew each other at Grey Advertising, which handled the Ohrbach's department-store account. Mr. Ohrbach was not happy with Grey and told Bill that he was taking the business to another agency. Mr. Ohrbach strongly suggested that Bernbach launch his own agency with Ohrbach's as its first client. Ohrbach even agreed to pay for all the work in advance, which enabled Doyle and Dane and Bernbach to pay their initial bills.

It's worth a moment to look into the relationship between N. M. Ohrbach and Bill Bernbach. They were such formative days for Bill and the new agency. According to Bill, N.M. was "distrusting," "uneducated," "insecure," and "big." Bill, of course, was none of these. But Ohrbach was a brute of an entrepreneur, and Bernbach made Ohrbach's cash registers ring.

Bill loved to talk about the closeness between them. But he also loved to tell about an Ohrbach's board meeting (Bill always attended these) at which Ohrbach, a classic Leo, demanded to know the astrological signs of everyone at the table.

"As each person announced his sign, he [Ohrbach] just glowed in that wonderful light of being the only one who was a Leo. And he got to me and asked, 'When were *you* born?' and I said, 'August 13.' 'August 13?' He looked down at me and said, *'You're a Leo?'* And I knew what he meant was 'How could you do this to me? You're destroying the image of a Leo!'"

At least some of the steel in Bill's blue eyes was hammered in the Ohrbach forge. And so was some of the most arresting, effective advertising of all time.

Ohrbach's was transformed from an unfashionable store in an unfashionable part of town to a "high fashion at low prices" boutique that attracted the attention of such people as the Rockefellers and drew "high fashion" coverage from *Life* magazine.

The beginning had begun.

I found out
about
Joan

The way she talks, you'd think she was in Who's Who. Well! I found out what's what with *her*. Her husband own a bank? Sweetie, not even a bank *account*. Why, that palace of theirs has wall-to-wall *mortgages!* And that car? Darling, that's horsepower, *not* earning power. They won it in a fifty-cent raffle! Can you imagine? And those clothes! Of course she *does* dress divinely. But really...a mink stole, and Paris suits, and all those dresses...on *his* income? Well darling, I found out about that too. I just happened to be going her way and *I saw Joan come out of Ohrbach's!'*

Ohrbach's

© 1958 by Ohrbach's Inc.

34TH ST. OPP. EMPIRE STATE BLDG. · **NEWARK** MARKET & HALSEY · **"A BUSINESS IN MILLIONS, A PROFIT IN PENNIES"**

I hate Ohrbach's!

I tell you, I'm fed up! It's just Ohrbach's, Ohrbach's, Ohrbach's every doggone day! She never has time for me any more. I want to romp in the park? *"Sorry, darling, Mommy must go to Ohrbach's for that mad little hat!"* I'm panting to be with old friends down at the plug? *"Not today, sweets. I must run to Ohrbach's. They've got the most* *divine pointy shoes!"* And trees? *"It'll have to wait, lamby. Ohrbach's has the darlingest dress. I simply must dash!"* Oh sure, she'll buy me more bones with the money she saves. Bones . . . to a fellow who's starving for *love!* Now I ask you, what kind of life *is this* for a dog? You know what *I* think? I think Ohrbach's was invented by *cats!*

Ohrbach's

We regret to inform you your school stuff is ready at Ohrbach's

Maybe you can't face it happily. But at least *face* it. You'll need slacks. Jeans. A rugby shirt. A coat with leather trim. Maybe even an Italian mohair sweater. If you've got a sister, she'll need an A-shape coat, something in fake fur, a skimmer, and the ski look for when it's cold. At Ohrbach's you'll find it all, beautifully made, in huge assortments ...at prices so low, you can afford what you need from now till school lets out. Come in; get it over with. We may not be able to make you look happy. But with clothes like these, we'll darn well make you look *smart*.
THE KIDS' SHOPS AT OHRBACH'S

New York: 34th St. Open Mon., Thurs., Fri. till 9. Newark: Market & Halsey. Open Mon., Wed., Fri., till 9. Westbury, L. I.: At the Raceway. Open Mon., Wed., Thurs., Fri., till 9:30; Tues. & Sat. till 6.

LIBERAL TRADE-IN

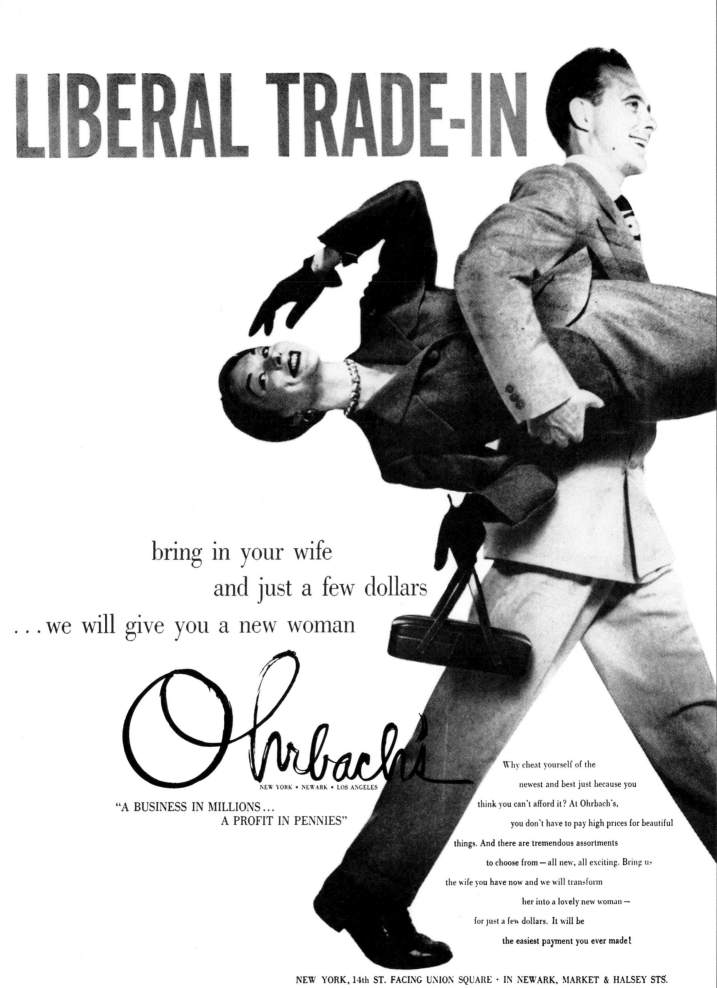

bring in your wife
and just a few dollars
...we will give you a new woman

Ohrbach's

NEW YORK · NEWARK · LOS ANGELES

"A BUSINESS IN MILLIONS...
A PROFIT IN PENNIES"

Why cheat yourself of the
newest and best just because you
think you can't afford it? At Ohrbach's,
you don't have to pay high prices for beautiful
things. And there are tremendous assortments
to choose from — all new, all exciting. Bring us
the wife you have now and we will transform
her into a lovely new woman —
for just a few dollars. It will be
the easiest payment you ever made!

NEW YORK, 14th ST. FACING UNION SQUARE · IN NEWARK, MARKET & HALSEY STS.

It's in,
but maybe
you shouldn't
be in it.

Some girls look sensational in hot pants. Front, back and sideways. So for those gorgeous girls Ohrbach's has an assortment of stylish hot pants and warm pants. All at Ohrbach's fabulously low prices.

But no one style is right for everybody. And a girl who looks absolutely divine in one outfit can look positively dreadful in another.

That's why Ohrbach's has so many thousands of fashions to choose from. We know there's a right look for everyone, and when you come into our store we want to be sure you'll find the one that's right for you. And at a price you can afford. At Ohrbach's, we believe that it isn't right if it isn't right for you.

OHRBACH'S Where you always find the right fashion and the price that's right for you.

"Playing it safe can be the most dangerous thing in the world, because you're presenting people with an idea they've seen before, and you won't have impact."

Levy's

Bill always insisted that the best way to get new business was to do a brilliant job for the clients you already had.

He believed this even when DDB had only one client—Ohrbach's. (In fact, DDB didn't put a new business presentation together for more than twenty years. During most of that time, Bill, Ned, Joe Daly, and several others *schlepped* a tattered black bag full of samples to new business meetings. By 1970, using this precarious method, the agency was billing about $280 million.)

The phone rang, as Bill predicted it would, and the caller was Whitey Ruben, a man who had just taken over the mainly bankrupt Levy's Bakery.

A $50,000 budget didn't buy much advertising, even then. But it was worth a try, especially since Levy's was such a good product. Part of its goodness lay in the fact that Levy's wasn't soft and squooshy, as other packaged breads were. People thought (and still think) that squeezing packaged bread is a test of freshness. Bill understood that the ingredients in Levy's bread and Levy's baking methods produced a loaf that wasn't squooshy at all.

And so the first campaign for Levy's asked readers the question "Are you buying a bed or a bread?" The question gave the advertising copy a chance to explain how and why Levy's was a quality product.

In less than a year, bankruptcy stopped being a problem, and Levy's advertising was accurately able to claim, "New York is eating it up." It would have been the wrong advertising a year earlier because it would not have been the truth. It was the right advertising at the time because it *was* the truth and people knew it.

By sheer chance, Bill was at a media meeting at which it was very nearly decided to put all of Levy's budget into the New York *Post*. When Bill asked why, the media director answered that research showed that the *Post* had an 80 percent Jewish circulation.

It made perfect sense. But not to Bill.

"Look," he said, "Levy's bread is sliced and put into waxed paper and delivered as quickly as possible, but it can't have the same taste as bread from the Jewish bakery on the corner. Why don't we put all the money into the *World Telegram*? They have very little Jewish circulation and their readers won't be able to make the comparison."

The idea that "You don't have to be Jewish to love Levy's" comes relentlessly from that point of view.

But even Whitey Ruben, by now a confirmed DDB devotee, had some trouble with Bill's suggestion that the product's name be changed from Levy's Real Rye to Levy's Real Jewish Rye. "Why should we put Jewish in it?" Whitey wanted to know. "There are are still lots of anti-Semitic people around. Why rub their noses in it?"

Bill said, "For God's sake, your name is Levy's. They're not going to mistake you for High Episcopalian!"

The "You don't have to be Jewish to love Levy's" poster campaign ran for many years in the New York City subways. Bookstores and poster shops sold countless copies of the posters to people everywhere. The words became part of the language. The appeal was universal, and Levy's is still an important brand name.

DDB never made a substantial amount of money with Levy's, but it didn't matter. The point was made and the phone kept ringing.

You don't have to be Jewish

to love Levy's
real Jewish Rye

You don't have to be Jewish

to love Levy's
real Jewish Rye

You don't have to be Jewish

to love Levy's
real Jewish Rye

"Imitation can be commercial suicide."

"You've got to live with your product. You've got to get steeped in it. You've got to get saturated with it. You must get to the heart of it. Indeed, if you have not crystallized into a single purpose, a single theme, what you want to tell the reader, you *cannot* be creative."

El Al
Israel Airlines

f you were traveling by air between the United States and Europe in 1957, El Al would not have been your first choice of an airline. It was virtually unknown.

On the other hand, if you were a well-known airline looking for an advertising agency in 1957, Doyle Dane Bernbach would not have been your first choice either. For the same reason.

It was DDB's brashness that brought the agency to El Al's attention. Bill took the small account, not only because it was new business (and *airline* business, at that) but because "it was like helping Israel."

El Al had just put the jet-prop Bristol Britannia into transatlantic service. It was exclusive to El Al, but, more important, it had an advantage: El Al could fly nonstop across the Atlantic without refueling at Goose Bay, Labrador, or Gander, Newfoundland.

The first advertisement for El Al, the "torn ocean," may be our best example of pure Bernbach: The words and pictures are stunning and inseparable, the advantage to the customer is piercingly clear and unforgettable, presented in a way that no one could pass by.

The ad ran once; it was enough.

El Al never spent great sums of money, but over the years its advertising was noticed more, respected more, perhaps even loved more than that of its richer competitors. Much to the wonderment and chagrin of those competitors, it also filled more seats.

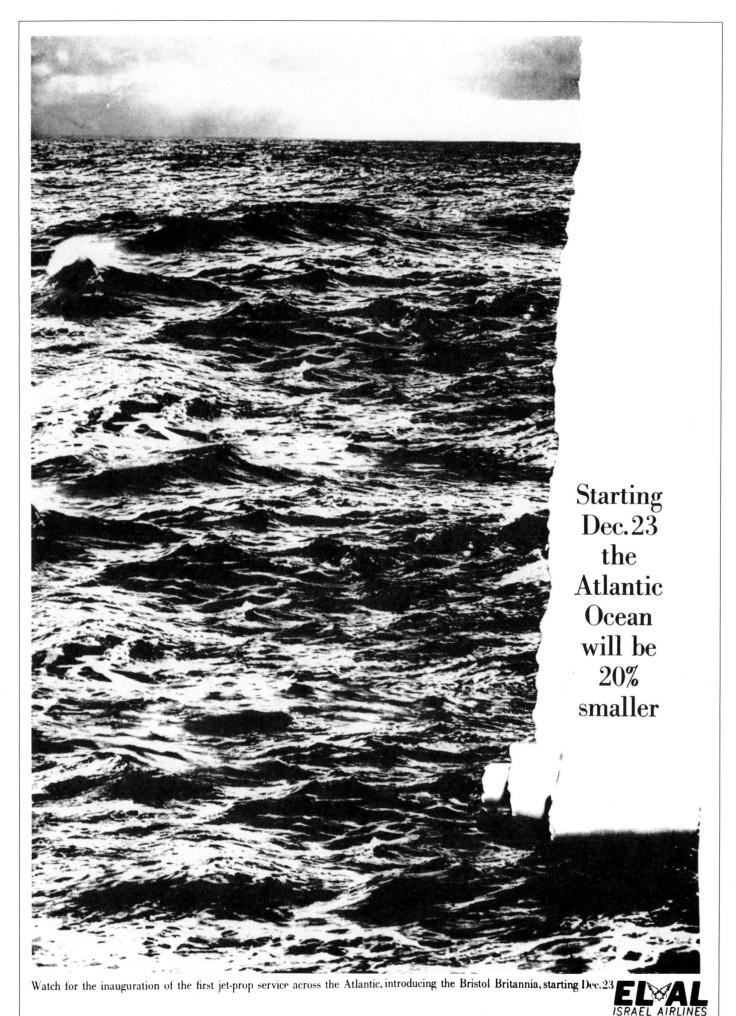

Starting
Dec. 23
the
Atlantic
Ocean
will be
20%
smaller

Watch for the inauguration of the first jet-prop service across the Atlantic, introducing the Bristol Britannia, starting Dec. 23

EL AL
ISRAEL AIRLINES

See your travel agent or El Al Israel Airlines, 610 Fifth Avenue, New York 20, N. Y., Plaza 1-4800

NO GOOSE

NO GANDER

No refueling stops at Goose Bay, Labrador or Gander, Newfoundland when you fly El Al jet-prop Britannia between New York and London or Paris. It's the only jet-powered airliner that makes it non-stop regularly across the Atlantic. Book El Al Britannia to London, Paris, Rome, Zurich, Athens, Tel Aviv. See your travel agent or **EL AL ISRAEL AIRLINES,** 610 Fifth Ave., New York 20, PLaza 1-7500.

My son, the pilot.

by Tillie Katz

Believe me.

I'm not saying this just because he's my only son.

But who ever thought a boy from Jacksonville, Florida would grow up to be the Chief Pilot for a whole airline?

It's funny, but Bill wasn't even interested in flying when he was young. Which was all right with me. Frankly, it made me a little nervous even when he played football.

Then something got into him. Just when we all thought he was going into some nice business, he enlisted in the Air Corps.

Pretty soon, he was a group commander with the 8th Air Force in Europe. By the time he came home, it was *Captain* Katz.

With a Distinguished Flying Cross, if you please.

Afterwards, it was flying, flying, flying.

I don't know if you could call him a pioneer or anything, but he was right there when EL AL was only a tiny little airline.

And now? Now you can call him Chief Pilot.

And does he keep an eye on that airline!

Sometimes I think he worries about it too much.

Do you know how many miles he's flown? Over 2 million! Do you know how long he's spent in the air? Over 12 thousand hours!

But if that's what it takes to make the airline so good, that's what he does.

The other pilots even tell a joke on him. They say he only comes down to collect his pay.

But *I* know better. I have two beautiful grandchildren who live in Israel with Bill and my daughter-in-law.

They come to see me now and then, but I wish I could spoil them more often. It's a good thing they have Bill for a father. He spoils everybody. Except himself.

So if you fly on EL AL and see him, tell him I said to dress warm.

We don't take off until everything is Kosher.

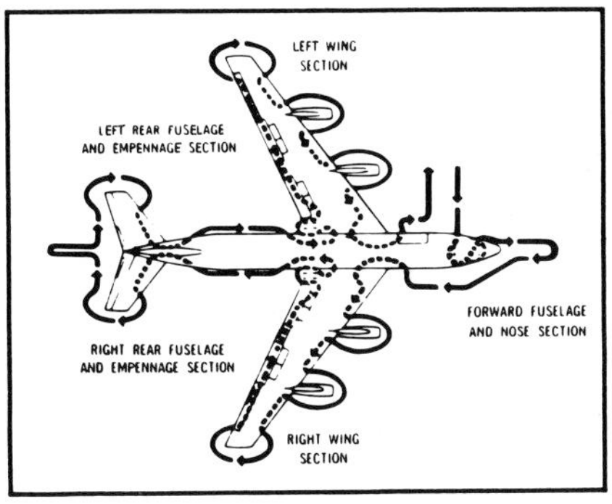

We spend more time walking than flying.

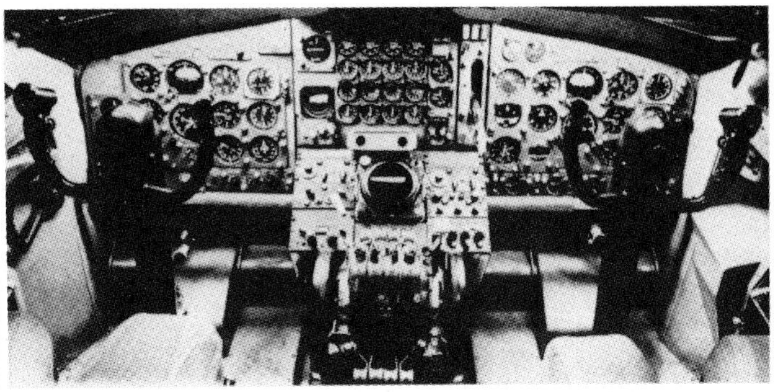
We check 597 controls...

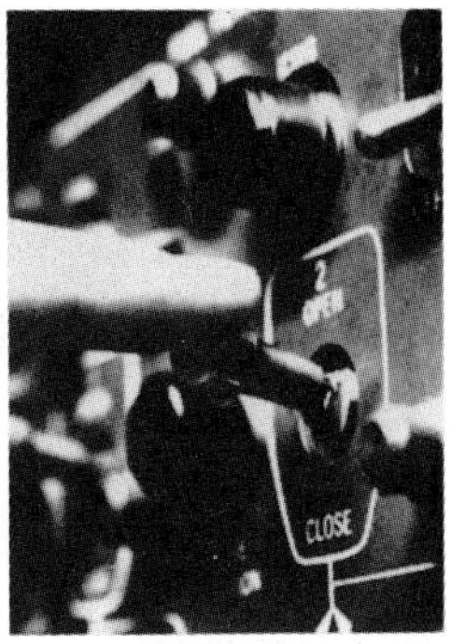

...one at a time

Kosher is sort of slang for "A.O.K."
Literally, it means "fitting and proper" in Hebrew.

And we take it very literally indeed.

Before we let one of our Boeing 707's off the ground, our crews do some fancy footwork to make sure that everything is just so.

To begin with, the ground crew takes a nice long walk all around the plane. Every inch of the wings, the fuselage and the engines gets scrutinized.

The things that are supposed to be open are opened.

The things that are supposed to be closed are closed.

Every item on a very long checklist must be initialed one by one, and the man who checks the checker must sign the completed form.

When the walk is over, the work has only begun.

One member of the ground crew goes into the cockpit to test all the controls. Another man stays outside to see what happens.

They speak to each other in a language all their own. When the man inside turns the control wheel to the right, the man outside says, "Left tabs up, left inboard ailerons down, left spoilers down, right tabs down, right inboard ailerons up, right spoilers up."

There are even tests to test the tests. Horns blow and lights light to show that things are working properly.

And if something isn't Kosher, everything stops until everything is.

If you took care of your car this carefully once a month, it would probably last forever.

Every EL AL jet gets the full treatment twice a day.

Meanwhile, there's the little matter of whipping up 3 square meals for 152 guests of this flying hotel.

What a job that is! Especially when you can't run out to the store if you're missing something at the last minute.

So we make sure that there's a little extra of everything; it hurts us to think of anyone going away hungry or thirsty.

We stock more than a dozen kinds of liquor on board; plus cigars, cigarettes, playing cards, olives, onions and cherries.

There's almost no end to the variety of things: from diapers to 2 sizes of doilies to 3 sizes of paper cups.

We even have 2 kinds of toothpicks: 1 kind for picking hors d'oeuvres and the other kind for picking teeth.

All of which brings us to the basic definition of Kosher that has to do with food.

Since we're the Israeli airline, we cook in the great Jewish tradition.

And the great Jewish tradition includes some tasty morsels (like matzo ball soup, kreplach, and gefilte fish) that are usually served only on festive occasions.

But we figure that an EL AL trip is a festive occasion all by itself, so we go all out and bend the rule a little by serving them every day.

Actually, the dietary laws can get pretty involved, but what it boils (or broils or roasts) down to is that we don't mix meat and dairy products during the same meal.

So there won't be any butter for your bread with the sumptuous roast beef, and there won't be cream with your coffee afterward.

On the other hand, when breakfast comes, you'll find gobs of butter to go with your lox, bagels and cream cheese, enough milk to bathe in, and all the cream you want for your coffee.

Above all, you get to fly with a bunch of enthusiastic people who don't have to work at being hospitable because that's the way they were brought up.

And you can be doubly sure that everything's Kosher. Inside the plane and inside you.

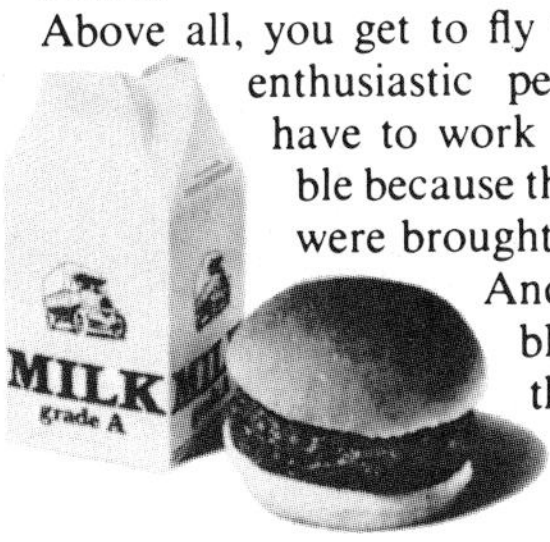

Hold it! Something isn't Kosher.

The Airline of Israel

For more information contact your travel agent or EL AL Israel Airlines, 8 South Michigan Ave., Chicago, Ill. 60603 (312) 236-3745.
For information on travel in Israel contact the Israel Government Tourist Office at 5 South Wabash, Chicago, Ill.

We've been in the travel business a long time.

In the beginning, it was sink or swim. We swam.

Until about 15 years ago when we started to fly.

In 1948, we had one used DC-4, two ex-war aces and plenty of doubts.

Now we have a whole fleet of new Boeing 707 and 720-B jets, plus a multitude of pilots (including one named Noah) and no more doubts.

We fly one of the world's longest non-stop flights: New York to Tel Aviv. The shorter EL AL non-stop flights (New York to London, Paris and Rome) are simply milk-and-honey runs to us.

One thing in particular that tickles us is that nobody notices when an EL AL jet puts down in Athens or Zurich or Istanbul.

It's absolutely routine.

We fly to all the places in the world

that you would expect: Brussels, Vienna, Munich, Amsterdam, Frankfurt.

And we also fly to some other places that you might not expect: Teheran, Nairobi and Nicosia, for instance.

At close to 600 miles an hour, there are very few places we can't get you to in 6 or 7 hours.

Think where we could get you in 40 days and 40 nights.

EL AL

Want an arkful of free facts? Write today, to: El Al Israel Airlines, Dept. 11, 610 5th Ave., New York 20, N.Y.

"It's not just what you say that stirs people. It's the way that you say it."

"Properly practiced creativity *must* result in greater sales more economically achieved. Properly practiced creativity can lift your claims out of the swamp of sameness and make them accepted, believed, persuasive, urgent."

Volkswagen

Volkswagen advertising is unique in the history of automobile advertising, if not all advertising. Its tone, style, wit, irreverence have been imitated, mimicked, swiped, copied, misunderstood, and admired more than any campaign before or since.

It was created by colorful people at Doyle Dane Bernbach and at Volkswagen of America, and in fact, it *created* colorful people by virtue of their association with it.

It was the DDB shot that is still heard around the world.

It is the classic story of a client with limited funds and unlimited vision, with faith in a wonderful product, who came to Bernbach's agency.

Bill saw the Volkswagen car for what it was: honest, simple, reliable, sensible, different. And he wanted the advertising to be that way too.

The temptations and pressures to do "mainstream" car advertising were considerable. Bill's resistance was greater. "The product. The product. Stay with the product." Simple.

When the VW campaign became established, there were other temptations at DDB: to out-VW VW itself, to be clever for its own sake. And Bill again: "The product. The product. Stay with the product."

Simple.

All the copiers and all the misunderstanders were doomed because they weren't selling Volkswagens and he was.

Simple:

In the end, the manfacturing philosophy and the advertising philosophy became one and the same. Volkswagen spoke with one voice throughout the world, and people everywhere recognized that voice.

Think small.

Our little car isn't so much of a novelty any more.

A couple of dozen college kids don't try to squeeze inside it.

The guy at the gas station doesn't ask where the gas goes.

Nobody even stares at our shape.

In fact, some people who drive our little flivver don't even think 32 miles to the gallon is going any great guns.

Or using five pints of oil instead of five quarts.

Or never needing anti-freeze.

Or racking up 40,000 miles on a set of tires.

That's because once you get used to some of our economies, you don't even think about them any more.

Except when you squeeze into a small parking spot. Or renew your small insurance. Or pay a small repair bill. Or trade in your old VW for a new one.

Think it over.

Lemon.

This Volkswagen missed the boat.

The chrome strip on the glove compartment is blemished and must be replaced. Chances are you wouldn't have noticed it; Inspector Kurt Kroner did.

There are 3,389 men at our Wolfsburg factory with only one job: to inspect Volkswagens at each stage of production. (3000 Volkswagens are produced daily; there are more inspectors than cars.)

Every shock absorber is tested (spot checking won't do), every windshield is scanned. VWs have been rejected for surface scratches barely visible to the eye.

Final inspection is really something! VW inspectors run each car off the line onto the Funktionsprüfstand (car test stand), tote up 189 check points, gun ahead to the automatic brake stand, and say "no" to one VW out of fifty.

This preoccupation with detail means the VW lasts longer and requires less maintenance, by and large, than other cars. (It also means a used VW depreciates less than any other car.)

We pluck the lemons; you get the plums.

This we change.

Now you can see for yourself where we make most of our changes. Way down deep.

Every part you can see (and every part you can't see) has been changed again and again and again.

But we never change the Volkswagen without a reason. And the only reason is to make it even better.

When we do make a change, we try to make the new part fit older models, too.

So you'll find that many VW parts are interchangeable from one year to the next.

Which is why it's actually easier to get parts for a VW than for many domestic cars.

This we don't.

And why VW service is as good as it is.

The same principle holds good for the beetle shape.

We made the rear window bigger one year so you could see other people better. We made the tail lights bigger last year so other people could see you better. But nothing drastic. Any Volkswagen hood still fits any

VW ever made. So does any fender.

And, in case you hadn't noticed, every VW still looks like every other VW.

Which may turn out to be the nicest thing of all about the car.

It doesn't go in one year and out the other.

"The difference between the forgettable and
the enduring is artistry."

The green fender came
    off a '58.
The blue hood came
    off a '59.
The beige fender came
    off a '64.
The turquoise door came
    off a '62.
Most VW parts
    are interchangeable
    from one year to the next.
That's why parts
    are so easy to get.

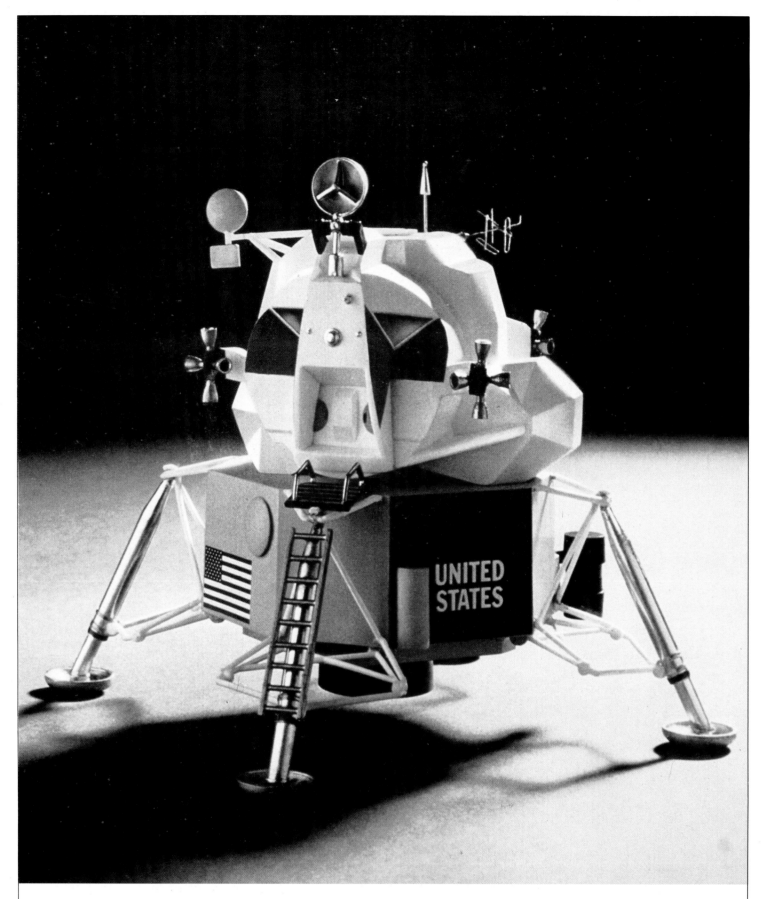

It's ugly, but it gets you there.

A new American plant.

After 27 years (and nearly 6 million VWs) in the U.S.A., we feel enough at home here to make a home here.

So we've opened a factory in Westmoreland, Pennsylvania, to make VW Rabbits as fast and as well as we know how.

Over the past years, you've found that we make good products. Over the coming years, you'll find that we make good corporate citizens, too.

Long ago, someone said, "I don't want an imported car. I want a Volkswagen."

How wunderbar that it turned out to be true.

Save water.

Presented by Volkswagen, the car with the air-cooled engine that doesn't use any.

"It was the only thing to do after the mule died."

Three years back, the Hinsleys of Dora, Missouri, had a tough decision to make.

To buy a new mule.

Or invest in a used bug.

They weighed the two possibilities.

First there was the problem of the bitter Ozark winters. Tough on a warm-blooded mule. Not so tough on an air-cooled VW.

Then, what about the eating habits of the two contenders? Hay vs. gasoline.

As Mr. Hinsley puts it: "I get over eighty miles out of a dollar's worth of gas and I get where I want to go a lot quicker."

Then there's the road leading to their cabin. Many a mule pulling a wagon and many a conventional automobile has spent many an hour stuck in the mud.

As for shelter, a mule needs a barn. A bug doesn't. "It just sets out there all day and the paint job looks near as good as the day we got it."

Finally, there was maintenance to think about. When a mule breaks down, there's only one thing to do: Shoot it.

 But if and when their bug breaks down, the Hinsleys have a Volkswagen dealer only two gallons away.

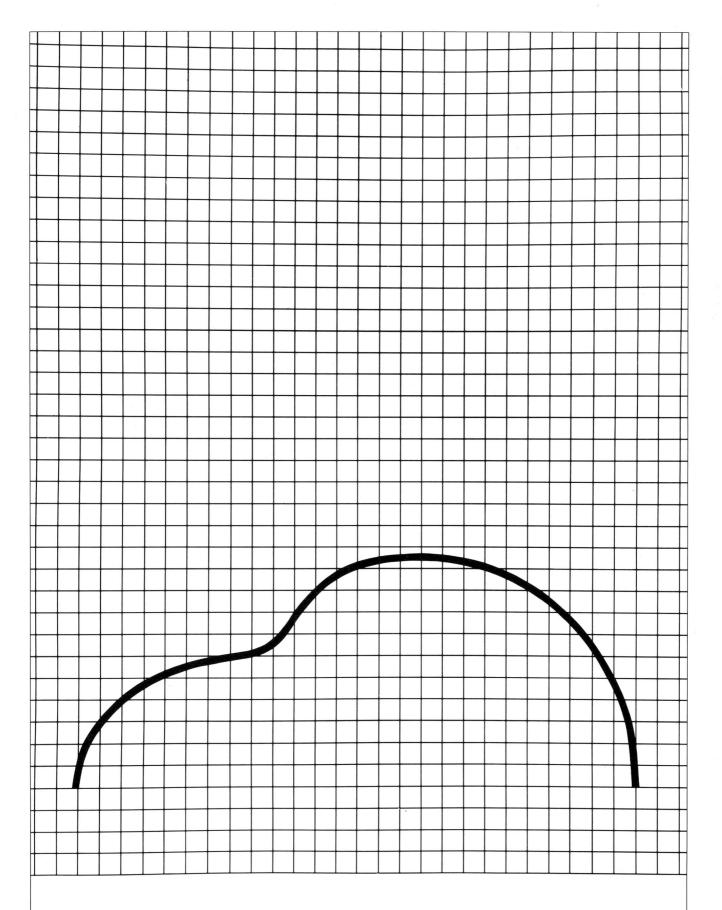

Is the economy trying to tell you something?

There are no real Volkswagen taxis. But there is one very good fake.

Think it over, New York, Chicago, San Francisco.

We drove our Volkswagen taxi through town on the way to get its picture taken.

And did we stop traffic!

You'd think it was the first sensible thing people had ever seen. And maybe it was.

A VW is 4 feet shorter than other cabs.

So a whole fleet of them is as good as getting miles of extra streets for free.

Because they're shorter, VWs get out of the way quicker. So traffic doesn't get all balled up while some lady hunts for a 5c tip.

The people who'd run Volkswagens could buy a lot more cabs for their money and run each one for a lot less, too.

They wouldn't need antifreeze in winter and they could forget about boiling over in summer; the VW engine is air-cooled.

Above all, the two passengers and the driver of a VW cab would have more fun than any other three people in town.

It may sound peculiar to you to stand on a corner and yell, "Volkswagen!"

But it sounds beautiful to us.

Got a lot to carry? Get a box.

Now add a few seats. Say 8.

Make an aisle so you can walk to the back.

Cut a hole in the roof to let the sun in.

Windows? At least 23. Doors? 5 should do.

Paint it up and what have you got?

The whole idea behind the Volkswagen Station Wagon.

© 1962 VOLKSWAGEN OF AMERICA, INC.

Or buy a Volkswagen.

That's about the size of it.

That special paint job is to make it perfectly clear that our Station Wagon is only 9 inches longer than our Sedan.

Yet it carries almost a ton of anything you like. (About twice as much as you can get into wagons that are 4 feet longer.)

Or eight solid citizens, with luggage.

Or countless kids, with kid stuff.

The things you never think about are worth thinking about, too.

You never worry about freezing or boiling; the rear engine is air-cooled.

You can expect about 24 miles per gallon and about 30,000 miles on your tires.

And you can forget about going out of style next year; next year's model will

look the same.

The most expensive VW Station Wagon costs $2,655.* It comes in red and white or grey and white or green and white.

And you won't ever have to go around painting sedans on it to show how small it is.

Just park.

Do you have the right kind of wife for it?

Can your wife bake her own bread?

Can she get a kid's leg stitched and not phone you at the office until it's all over?

Find something to talk about when the TV set goes on the blink?

Does she worry about the Bomb?

Make your neighbors' children wish that she were their mother?

Will she say "Yes" to a camping trip after 50 straight weeks of cooking?

Let your daughter keep a pet snake in the back yard?

Invite 13 people to dinner even though she only has service for 12?

Name a cat "Rover"?

Live another year without furniture and take a trip to Europe instead?

Let you give up your job with a smile?

And mean it?

Congratulations.

The '51 '52 '53 '54 '55 '56 '57 '58 '59 '60 '61 Volkswagen.

Ever since we started making Volkswagens, we've put all our time and effort into the one basic model.

You can see we've had lots of practice.

We've learned to make every part of the VW fit every other part so well, the finished car is practically air-tight.

The engine is so carefully machined and assembled, you can drive a brand new VW at top speed all day.

We don't make changes lightly. And never to make the VW look different; only to make it work better.

When we do make a change, we go out of our way to make the new part fit older Volkswagens, too.

With this result: An authorized Volkswagen dealer can repair any year's Volkswagen, even the earliest. (Why not? They use mostly interchangeable parts!)

If you had to decide between a car that went out of style every year or two and a car that never did, which would it be?

$1.02 a pound.

A new Volkswagen costs $1,595.*

But that isn't as cheap as it sounds. Pound for pound, a VW costs more than practically any car you can name.

Actually, that isn't too surprising when you look into it.

Not many cars get as much put into them as a Volkswagen.

The hand work alone is striking.

VW engines are put together by hand. One by one.

And every engine is tested twice: once when it's still an engine and again when it's part of the finished car.

A Volkswagen gets painted 4 times and sanded by hand between each coat

Even the roof lining is hand-fitted.

You won't find a nick or a dimple or a blob of glue anywhere because VW isn't above rejecting a piece of car (or a whole car) if it has to.

So you can see why a Volkswagen is so expensive when you figure it by the pound.

It's something to think about.

Particularly if you haven't bought a Volkswagen because you thought they didn't cost enough.

AUTHORIZED
DEALER

33 years later, he got the bug.

We're glad that most people don't wait 33 years to buy their first Volkswagen.

But Albert Gillis did, and maybe he had the right idea all along.

He didn't buy a new car for 33 years because he didn't happen to need one.

He and his 1929 Model A Ford did just fine by each other.

He always did his own repairs and even jacked it up at night to save the tires.

When he needed a new car last year, he went out and bought a Volkswagen.

"I heard they hold up," he explained. Does he like the VW?

Mr. Gillis is 78, a Justice of the Peace, and not given to hasty decisions.

"Your inspectors sure do a good job of inspecting," was as far as he would go.

But he did mention that he and Mrs. Gillis took a trip for their 54th anniversary.

They drove 6,750 miles and spent $62 on gas and 55¢ on oil.

"I didn't think they were supposed to burn oil," he said.

"All of us who professionally use the mass media are the shapers of society. We can vulgarize that society. We can brutalize it. Or we can help lift it onto a higher level."

"Today everybody is talking 'Creativity,' and, frankly, that's got me worried. I fear lest we keep the good taste and lose the sell. I fear all the sins we may commit in the name of 'Creativity.' I fear that we may be entering an age of phonies."

VW "Snow Plow"

1 Have you ever wondered how the man who drives the snow-plow drives *to* the snowplow?

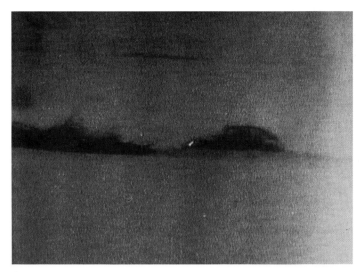

2

3 This one drives a Volkswagen.

4

5

6 So you can stop wondering.

VW "Funeral"

1 I, Max E. Mably, being of sound mind and body, do hereby bequeath the following:

2 To my wife, Rose, who spent money like there was no to-morrow, I leave 100 dollars and a calendar.

3 To my sons, Rodney and Victor, who spent every dime I ever gave them on fancy cars and fast women, I leave 50 dollars in dimes.

4 To my business partner, Jules, whose only motto was "Spend! Spend! Spend!" I leave Nothing! Nothing! Nothing!

5 Finally, to my nephew, Harold, who ofttimes said, "a penny saved is a penny earned," and who also ofttimes said, "Gee, Uncle Max, it sure pays to own a Volkswagen," I leave my entire fortune of 100 billion dollars.

6

1 The Volkswagen Karmann-Ghia is the most economical sports car you can buy.

2

3

4

5

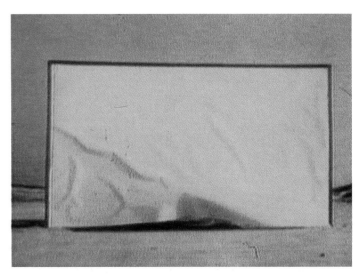

6 It's just not the most powerful.

1   And now the star of the 1949 Auto Show. The car of the future. The car the public wants. The all-new De Soto!

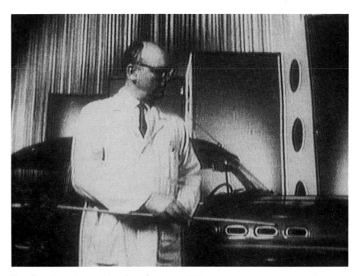

2   So there's no doubt about it. Next year every car in America will have holes in its side.

3   So the man to see if you're buying your next car for keeps is your nearby Packard dealer!

4   (singing) Longer, lower, wider . . . The '49 Hudson is the car for you!

5   So Volkswagen will constantly be changing, improving, and refining their car. Not necessarily to keep in style with the times, but to make a better car. Which means, to all of you, better mileage.

6   (VO) Of all the promises made at the 1949 Auto Show, we at Volkswagen kept ours.

Volkswagen "Keeping Up With The Kremplers"

1 Mr. Jones and Mr. Krempler were neighbors. They each had 3,000 dollars.

2 With his money, Mr. Jones bought himself a $3,000 car.

3 With his money, Mr. Krempler bought himself a new refrigerator, a new range, a new washer . . .

4 . . . a new dryer, a record player, two new television sets . . .

5 . . . *and* a brand new Volkswagen.

6 Now Mr. Jones is faced with that age-old problem . . . keeping up with the Kremplers.

VW "Baker"

1 (VO) Brooklyn, New York.

2 Baker: Uh! It doesn't fit. Uhh.
(VO) Excuse me. Why are you delivering that huge cake in a Volkswagen Rabbit?

3 Baker: Because it didn't fit in my big Ford wagon.
(VO) I don't understand.

4 Baker: Neither can I. I bought the wagon because it was big, and the Rabbit because it was small. Now the big car is smaller than the Rabbit, and the Rabbit is bigger than the big car. It's making me crazy.

5 (VO) What do you say about the Rabbit now?

6 Baker: Let them eat cake.

Avis

Bob Townsend, the president of the new and tiny Avis and a maverick, came around to see Bill Bernbach and offered DDB the Avis account. The maverick aspect of DDB attracted Townsend, and he got what he asked for. "OK," Bill said, "we'll take it. But you must do exactly what we recommend."

When Townsend saw the campaign, it may have been even more than he had asked for. But he was as good as his word and agreed to run the now-legendary "We try harder" Avis campaign.

Overnight, the campaign was seen, talked about, resultful. Avis was on the map.

People sometimes refer to the Avis advertising as the "We're only #2" campaign—a serious misunderstanding of how people work and why the Avis campaign worked.

"We're only #2" and *that's why* "We try harder" is more like it.

In today's marketingese, this is called "permission to believe." In Bill's day, it was called a damned good argument.

Before Bob Townsend saw the campaign, there was some research done by DDB to see whether people liked the advertising or not.

To some minds, the results were grim: Half the people who were asked didn't like the ads. "But half the people did," Bill said, "and that's the half we want. Let's go with it."

Typically, he was right. Avis flourished. But in this case, the two companies failed to see eye to eye on many issues. Bob Townsend left. Avis management changed several times.

DDB was fired, then hired again, then fired again.

But now, twenty years later, if you pick up any magazine in any country in the world where Avis rents cars, you will see the campaign running in very nearly its original form or with a deafening echo of it.

That's the way it goes sometimes.

Avis is only No.2 in rent a cars. So why go with us?

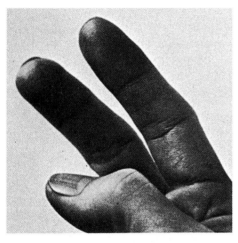

We try harder.

(When you're not the biggest, you have to.)

We just can't afford dirty ashtrays. Or half-empty gas tanks. Or worn wipers. Or unwashed cars. Or low tires. Or anything less than seat-adjusters that adjust. Heaters that heat. Defrosters that defrost.

Obviously, the thing we try hardest for is just to be nice. To start you out right with a new car, like a lively, super-torque Ford, and a pleasant smile. To know, say, where you get a good pastrami sandwich in Duluth.

Why?

Because we can't afford to take you for granted.

Go with us next time.

The line at our counter is shorter.

Avis can't afford dirty ashtrays.

Or to start you out without a full gas tank, a new car like a lively, super-torque Ford, a smile.
Why?
When you're not the biggest in rent a cars, you have to try harder.
We do.
We're only No. 2.

© 1963 AVIS, INC.

When you're only No. 2, you try harder. Or else.

Avis can't afford to relax.

Little fish have to keep moving all of the time. The big ones never stop picking on them.

Avis knows all about the problems of little fish.

We're only No. 2 in rent a cars. We'd be swallowed up if we didn't try harder.

There's no rest for us.

We're always emptying ashtrays. Making sure gas tanks are full before we rent our cars. Seeing that the batteries are full of life. Checking our windshield wipers.

And the cars we rent out can't be anything less than lively new super-torque Fords.

And since we're not the big fish, you won't feel like a sardine when you come to our counter.

We're not jammed with customers.

No. 2ism.
The Avis Manifesto.

We are in the rent a car business, playing second fiddle to a giant.

Above all, we've had to learn how to stay alive.

In the struggle, we've also learned the basic difference between the No. 1's and No. 2's of the world.

The No. 1 attitude is: "Don't do the wrong thing. Don't make mistakes and you'll be O.K."

The No. 2 attitude is: "Do the right thing. Look for new ways. Try harder."

No. 2ism is the Avis doctrine. And it works.

The Avis customer rents a clean, new Opel Rekord, with wipers wiping, ashtrays empty, gas tank full, from an Avis girl with smile firmly in place.

And Avis itself has come out of the red into the black.

Avis didn't invent No. 2ism. Anyone is free to use it.

No. 2's of the world, arise!

"Merely to let your imagination run riot, to dream unrelated dreams, to indulge in graphic acrobatics and verbal gymnastics, is *not* being creative. The creative person has harnessed his imagination. He has disciplined it so that every thought, every idea, every word he puts down, every line he draws, every light and shadow in every photograph he takes, make more vivid, more believable, more persuasive the original theme or product advantage he has decided he must convey."

Who do you think of first when you think of rent a cars? Certainly not Avis.

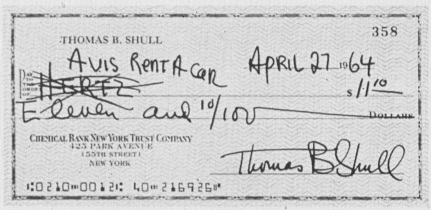

How one of our customers made out his check.

It must be nice to be a household word. Like Jell-O, Coke or Kodak.

But we're not. Avis is only No. 2 in rent a cars, and it's always the big fellow you think of first.

So we have to try harder. Hoping the people who stumble on us will come back for more.

(We probably have the world's most fussed-over Fords. Spick and span and nicely in tune.)

And when someone calls us by the wrong name, we turn the other cheek.

After all, it doesn't matter what you call us.

Just so you call.

© 1964 AVIS, INC.

n 1965 the Mobil Oil Corporation set aside a budget of $1 million to commemorate its one hundredth anniversary.

They wanted to talk to two advertising agencies: the people who were doing the Volkswagen campaign and the people who were doing the Avis campaign. Since they were the same people, there was only one meeting, but it was a historic one.

In the course of it, Rawleigh Warner, Jr., who was then chairman of Mobil, unveiled a poster that had been prepared in-house at Mobil and for which Mr. Warner had some obvious fondness. It looked like this:

M⊙bil 1865
1965

"What do you think of it, Mr. Bernbach?" asked Mr. Warner.

Bill studied it for a very long minute and said, "I think it means you died."

Nearly everyone did. But somehow DDB walked out with the assignment and walked in a few weeks later with the "We want you to live" campaign.

The advertising was genuinely helpful, in the public interest, totally credible, designed to point out the horrors of dangerous driving, with no product orientation at all.

The response was remarkable, and at first almost frightening. Tens of thousands of letters of gratitude, many of them asking for credit card applications (which the advertising never solicited), flooded Mobil's mailroom. It was a huge job simply to acknowledge all the mail and to assess the impact of what a relatively small advertising investment could produce.

After the one hundredth anniversary year, a grateful Mobil awarded its entire gasoline and oil advertising budget to DDB. And it seems fair to guess that the very forthright, outspoken advocacy advertising that Mobil does today took the "We want you to live" campaign as its inspirational model.

The advertising for Mobil gasoline has been singlemindedly helping to sell the "detergent gasoline" for nearly twenty years, and Mobil 1, "the oil that saves you gas," for more than a decade.

While the managements of both companies have changed and the creative teams have changed many times, the creative executions continue to be fresh and arresting and successful.

Fresh-killed chicken.

Bravo.

Let's hear it for the winner.

That's him lying there – the dead one.

Or is he the loser?

You can't tell. Not that it matters very much. Because in the idiot game of "chicken," winners and losers both die.

In the idiot game of "chicken," two cars speed straight for each other. Head on.

With luck, one car steers clear in the nick of time.

Without luck, neither car steers clear. And the winner and the loser are equally dead.

Some "game."

It took God Almighty to stop Abraham from making a blood sacrifice of his son.

What do you suppose it will take to make us stop sacrificing our children?

We who bear them in sterilized hospitals, stuff them with vitamins, educate them expensively, and then hand over the keys to the car and wait with our hearts in our mouths.

Too bad we educate them only to make a living and not to stay alive.

Because right now – this year – car accidents kill more young people than anything else. Including war. Including cancer. Including anything.

Yet we allow it.

Incredibly enough, fewer than half the young people who get drivers' licenses every year have passed a driver training course.

Which leaves well over 2 million (!) youngsters who get licenses every year without passing such a course.

And this is the price we pay: 13,200 young people between 15 and 24 died in automobile accidents in 1965. (The exact number for 1966 isn't in yet; it will probably be higher.)

It's a gruesome answer to the population explosion.

And if we all sit still about it, we ourselves are guilty of "chickening out."

Yet we mustn't frighten our youngsters; they're frightened enough.

We must teach them.

Does your school system have a driver training course?

Are there books in your school library or public library on driving? (Did you know such books exist? Do they know?)

Are the requirements for getting a driver's license in your state tough enough?

Are your radio and TV stations paying any attention to the problem? Your newspapers?

Does anyone in your community give awards for good driving? The PTA? Or the Boy Scouts? The Chamber of Commerce? The churches or synagogues?

What kind of driver are you yourself? Do you set a good example or a poor one?

Would your company insist on a driver training course before they'd hire someone?

Would your schools insist on a training course before they'd turn a youngster loose?

Would it help?

Yes, it would. Education works. Drivers in large truck fleets are trained to drive safely. And some of them have dropped accident rates to only about half that of the general public.

It would cost little or nothing to get these things going. And we haven't a minute to spare. It's blood that we have on our hands, not time.

We at Mobil sell gasoline and oil for our living to the living. Naturally, we'd like young people to grow up into customers. But for now we'd be happy if they'd simply grow up.

Mobil
We want you to live.

Till death us do part.

It may be beautiful to die for love in a poem.

But it's ugly and stupid to die for love in a car.

Yet how many times have you seen (or been) a couple more interested in passion than in passing? Too involved with living to worry about dying?

As a nation, we are allowing our young to be buried in tons of steel. And not only the reckless lovers—the just plain nice kids as well.

Everyone is alarmed about it. No one really knows what to do. And automobile accidents, believe it or not, continue to be the leading cause of death among young people between 15 and 24 years of age.

Parents are alarmed and hand over the keys to the car anyway.

Insurance companies are alarmed and charge enormous rates which deter no one.

Even statisticians (who don't alarm easily) are alarmed enough to tell us that by 1970, 14,450 young adults will die in cars each year.

(Just to put those 14,450 young lives in perspective, that is about 4 times the number of young lives we have lost so far in Viet Nam.)

Is it for this that we spent our dimes and dollars to all but wipe out polio? Is it for this that medical science conquered diphtheria and smallpox?

What kind of society is it that keeps its youngsters alive only long enough to sacrifice them on the highway?

Yet that is exactly what's happening. And it's incredible.

Young people should be the best drivers, not the worst.

They have the sharper eyes, the steadier nerves, the quicker reflexes. They probably even have the better understanding of how a car works.

So why?

Are they too dense to learn? Too smart to obey the obvious rules? Too sure of themselves? Too *un*-sure? Or simply too young and immature?

How can we get them to be old enough to be wise enough before it's too late?

One way is by insisting on better driver training programs in school. Or *after* school. Or after work. Or during summers.

By having stricter licensing requirements. By rewarding the good drivers instead of merely punishing the bad ones. By having uniform national driving laws (which don't exist today). By having radio and TV and the press deal more with the problem. By getting *you* to be less complacent.

Above all, by setting a decent example ourselves.

Nobody can stop young people from driving. And nobody should. Quite the contrary. The more exposed they become to sound driving techniques, the better they're going to be. (Doctors and lawyers "practice;" why not drivers?)

We at Mobil are not preachers or teachers. We sell gasoline and oil for a living and we want everyone to be a potential customer.

If not today, tomorrow. And we want everyone, young and old, to have his fair share of tomorrows. **Mobil**

We want you to live.

We lose
too many customers
this way.

Let's put it right on the table

We are not doing well as a nation in our fight to end highway killings.

This past Memorial Day it was predicted that at least 460 people would die. But we set a new record: 542 died instead.

We ought to be ashamed of ourselves.

Here we are, the richest, smartest country in the world. Yet our President is compelled to tell us that the "greatest problem before this nation—next to the war in Viet Nam—is the death and destruction . . . on our highways."

We are sorry to tell you that the worst is yet to come. More people die in traffic accidents in July and August than in any other two-month period.

Will you be on the road this July 4th weekend? Can you look yourself squarely in the eye and answer these questions?

Do you have enough brake fluid? Are your brakes adjusted? Do your stoplights work? Your directional signals? Do you have a bad tire? Does your horn blow? Is your steering O.K.? Your wheel alignment? Do your windshield wipers work? Is there a leak in your exhaust system?

Everything O.K.? Glad to hear it.

Now hear this.

Even if your car were in perfect shape, you could still be in terrible trouble. Almost 70% of all turnpike accidents have to do with drivers, not with cars.

In 41% of fatal accidents, the driver was drunk, drowsy, sleeping or simply not paying attention. In 22% of fatal accidents, the driver was just plain going too fast. And so on down the list until you get sick to the stomach.

Well, there it is. On the table.

You can be smart this weekend. Or you can be stupid. You can live this weekend. Or you can die.

We at Mobil are in the business of selling gasoline and oil. And we're very good at it. (We're the 5th largest industrial corporation in the United States.) But big as we are, we never forget that we make our living from the *living*. Everyone who drives can be a customer of ours. And we don't have a single customer to spare. **Mobil**

We want you to live.

Mobil Ten-Story Building

1 This demonstration is being brought to you by Mobil.

2 We are going to put a car on the roof of a ten-story building and then push it off to make a simple point.

3 If you drive at sixty miles an hour and hit something, it's exactly the same as driving off a ten-story building. And it will get you to exactly the same place.

4 The morgue.

5 When you drive fast, remember, this is how it is. But it doesn't have to be. We at Mobil hope you'll remember that fact. Our business is to sell you gasoline and oil, and we want you to be around to try them.

6 We want you to live.

Mobil "Cold Weather"

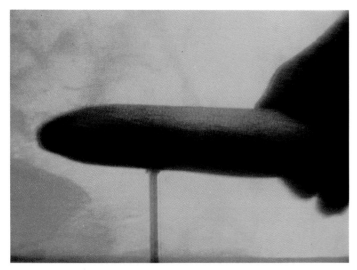

1   At thirty-five degrees below zero, this is what you can do with a banana.

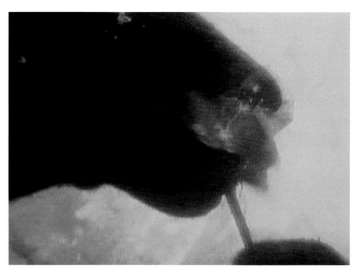

2   This is what happens to a freshly cut rose.

3   And this is premium motor oil.

4

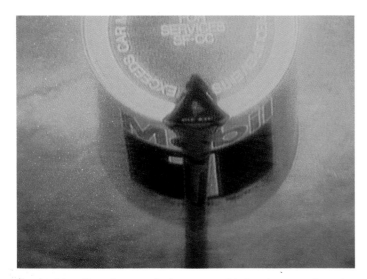

5   At thirty-five degrees below zero, this is what you can do with Mobil 1 Motor Oil.

6   Mobil 1. The oil that saves you gas. Helps get you going, even at thirty-five below.

Mobil "25,000 Miles"

1 You know what you can do with Mobil 1?

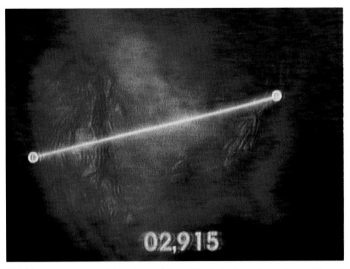

2 You can now drive from New York to Los Angeles without an oil change and back.

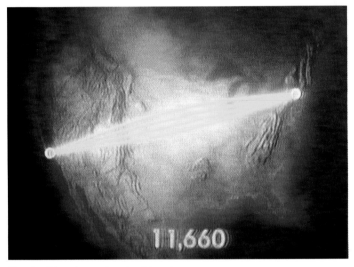

3 And back again. And back.

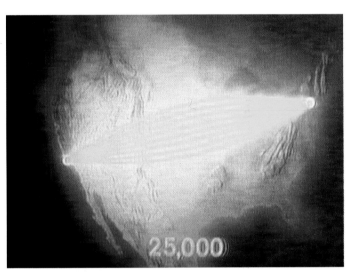

4 And back again. And back.

5 Twenty-five thousand miles without an oil change.

6 That's what you can do with Mobil 1.

Chivas Regal

Today, if your host serves you Chivas Regal, it says something important about both of you.

This was not always true.

The groundwork for turning Chivas Regal into "the Chivas Regal of Scotches" was laid even before Doyle Dane Bernbach got the account.

In their first meeting, Bill said to "Mr. Sam" Bronfman, "I think I ought to tell you that I will never know as much about your business as you do. How can I? You built it, you breathe it, you dream it. But you have to understand that I'm in a different business from you, even though it involves your product. And I know my business better than you do."

Mr. Bronfman's answer was, "You mean together we can do a great job? OK, you've got the account."

Having said that, Mr. Sam instantly took Bill to his own desk and opened a huge drawer, which was jammed with drawings and photographs of pedestals from the world over. And he said, "Bill, this is going to be a very easy assignment. All you have to do is put my bottle on top of one of these pedestals."

The lines were drawn. And in this case, there was an extra bit of irony that was yet to surface.

Mr. Bronfman correctly foresaw the trend to "lighter" alcoholic drinks, and he replaced the classic murky, dark green Chivas Regal bottle with one of clear glass.

Bernbach understood and agreed with the reason for the change, and so DDB's first ad for Chivas Regal carried this headline: "What idiot changed the Chivas Regal bottle?"

Bronfman was not a happy man. "But, Bill," he said, "we talked about pedestals."

Bernbach's answer was, "Yes, you mentioned the pedestals to me, but that's wrong. Why should somebody believe you if you, the father of that product, puts his own child on display? If somebody comes to you and says, 'I have the most brilliant son in the world,' you smile at him, you understand him, but you don't believe him. That's what you'd be doing with your product."

"Are you making me out to be a liar or something?" Bronfman exploded.

"No, I'm just telling you how people will read," Bernbach offered.

"Well, OK," Mr. Sam said. "But couldn't you at least say, 'What *genius* changed the Chivas Regal bottle?' "

The dark green bottle is long forgotten now. Countless teams of creative people at DDB have contributed to the campaign and, more important, to the idea that Chivas Regal is *the* status symbol in the world of Scotch whisky.

In fact, if all the people in the world who claim to drink Chivas actually did so, there would never be enough to go around.

the Chivas Regal bottle?

When the Chivas Regal people changed their bottle recently, they were ready for some protests.

Not a storm of outrage.

At first, it does seem outrageous.

Why change a classic bottle?

A magnificent dark green bottle. And an antique shield that seemed to come out of Sir Walter Scott.

"It's a wonder they kept the shape," muttered one Chivas Regal fan.

True, the shape is the same.

Still squat. Still jaunty.

Most important, the Scotch inside is still the same Chivas Regal.

Not a day younger than 12 years. "Goode olde whiskie is a

Old.

heavenly spirit."

Then why change the bottle to clear flint glass? Why lighten the antique shield?

Because we live in an age of confusions.

One minor confusion is "light" Scotch.

People think of "light" Scotch

New.

as light in color. Color has nothing to do with "lightness."

People think of "light" Scotch as "weakened" whisky. Not so. Almost all Scotch is the same 86 proof.

True lightness is actually the "smoothness" of Scotch.

A light Scotch will go down as easily as water. Or honey.

No "back bite." No gasp. No wince. No shudder.

Many people consider Chivas Regal the smoothest (or lightest) Scotch in the world.

Why?

Since 1786, Chivas Regal has been made with the "soft" Highland Scotch of Glenlivet. (This

is prize Scotch whisky.)

Extravagant sherry casks are still brought from Spain for ripening it. (Each costs over £35.)

Chivas Regal is still the same clear gold color it has always been.

This color is what warrants changing the bottle.

Many people have never tasted Chivas Regal, because its clear golden color never showed.

Handsome though it was, the old dark green bottle made Chivas Regal look dark.

Some people translated this as "heavy."

Many people never saw Chivas Regal in a restaurant or bar.

The old dark bottle and label almost hid it.

Same great Scotch inside.

No longer.

The new clear bottle offers an uninterrupted view of Chivas Regal.

And a warm welcome.

Think of it that way, and it's not so idiotic, is it?

It's kind of brilliant.

12-YEAR-OLD BLENDED SCOTCH WHISKY. 86 PROOF. GENERAL WINE AND SPIRITS CO., N.Y., N.Y.

Does Chivas Regal embarrass you?

If it does, it's all our fault.

Maybe, in trying to tell you what a really fine whisky it is, we over-played our hand.

It's possible we left you with the notion that you have to be a special kind of person to be at home with it.

You do.

You're that kind of person.

You want nothing but the best.

That's what Chivas is.

"A unique selling proposition is no longer enough.
Without a unique selling talent, it may die."

"To keep your ads fresh, you've got to keep yourself fresh.
Live in the current idiom and you will create in it. If you
follow and enjoy and are excited by the new trails in art,
in writing, in industry, in personal relationships . . .
whatever you do will naturally be of today."

Chivas Regal / 71

Give dad
an
expensive
belt.

12 YEARS OLD WORLDWIDE·
BLENDED SCOTCH WHISKY 86 PROOF·
GENERAL WINE & SPIRITS CO., NEW YORK, N.Y.

The Chivas Regal of Scotches.

12 YEARS OLD WORLDWIDE · BLENDED SCOTCH WHISKY · 86 PROOF · GENERAL WINE & SPIRITS CO., NEW YORK, N.Y.

I'll be home for Chivas.

Tsk, tsk.

After a party, the host is often faced with several almost-empty Scotch bottles.

And there's a natural tendency to consolidate the leftovers in a single bottle.

Guess whose.

Now we don't intend to comment on the morality of this. (We're kind of flattered that the Chivas Regal bottle should so often have the honor.)

But please don't. You're not fooling anyone. Anyone who knows Scotch, that is.

Chivas Regal is a very distinctive whisky. Many people consider it the smoothest of all Scotches.

It's made with prize Glenlivet whiskies from the oldest distillery in the Scottish Highlands.

And every drop is aged 12 years.

Newcomers ask us how much training it takes to tell Chivas Regal from the others.

Order a glass at your local bar. Sip it, neat.

That should do the trick.

12-YEAR-OLD BLENDED SCOTCH WHISKY · 86 PROOF
GENERAL WINE AND SPIRITS CO., NEW YORK, N.Y.

This bottle is ½ empty.

This bottle is ½ full.

If it happens to be your bottle of Chivas that reaches the halfway mark, you'll probably feel it's half empty.

Whereas, if you're visiting a friend and his bottle reaches the same point, you can relax, knowing that it's still half full.

Polaroid

D r. Edwin Land, the genius who invented Polaroid instant photography, felt, perhaps instinctively, that Polaroid's advertising wasn't getting his message across.

It may have been part of his genius.

Although Doyle Dane Bernbach was barely five years old and billing only $750,000 a year, Dr. Land knew the agency's work and was attracted by it.

Polaroid had been running advertising that was cluttered with a number of different typefaces, some in reverse. There were arrows all over the place and unattractive pictures of the camera and by the camera.

The look of the pages said: "Cheap. Novelty. Gimmick."

The price ($100) said: "Expensive."

The two didn't match. The message was in conflict with itself.

Immediately, the look of the advertising was changed. Polaroid was selling pictures, so the advertising showed big, beautiful pictures in unadorned, totally straightforward ads.

But of course the magic of Polaroid was *instant* pictures. And live television was the perfect medium to communicate that magic.

So DDB began a series of sixty-second commercials on live television talk shows and entertainment shows. Extremely popular and totally believable personalities such as Garry Moore, Steve Allen, Jack Paar, and Johnny Carson did live Polaroid commercials, which showed applauding audiences the wonders of instant photography. Even when a picture failed to develop successfully (which happened on a few occasions), the personality simply took another picture and said, "See? You know instantly whether or not you've got the shot!"

The use of personalities extended far beyond the days of live television. Stars such as Candice Bergen, Jane Fonda, James Garner, Danny Kaye, and Sir Laurence Olivier all appeared in Polaroid commercials. In the case of Mariette Hartley, who appeared in Polaroid spots with James Garner for six years, Polaroid made *her* a star.

As live television turned to film and tape, Polaroid commercials did, too.

The magic of Polaroid photography had been well established. And now, Polaroid advertising dealt with the *why* of instant photography. In a series of wonderfully well-cast, well-directed, hauntingly emotional commercials, the benefits of instant pictures were shown to moist-eyed audiences who responded by buying millions of Polaroid cameras and more millions of packs of Polaroid film.

Although Doyle Dane Bernbach lost the Polaroid account in 1984, it is widely acknowledged that for thirty years Polaroid and DDB "wrote the book" on knowing what to do and when and how to do it.

FIRST SHOWING OF A NEW POLAROID LAND FILM. This is an enlargement of an actual 60-second picture of Louis Armstrong. It was taken with a new film, just introduced, which is twice as sharp as the previous film.

With this latest development, the Polaroid Land Camera not only gives you pictures in 60 seconds, but pictures of exceptional clarity and brilliance. Polaroid Land Cameras start at $72.75. The new film can be identified by a star on the box.

10 good little Indians.

"Our job is to sell our clients' merchandise . . . not ourselves. Our job is to kill the cleverness that makes us shine instead of the product. Our job is to simplify, to tear away the unrelated, to pluck out the weeds that are smothering the product message."

Polaroid / 81

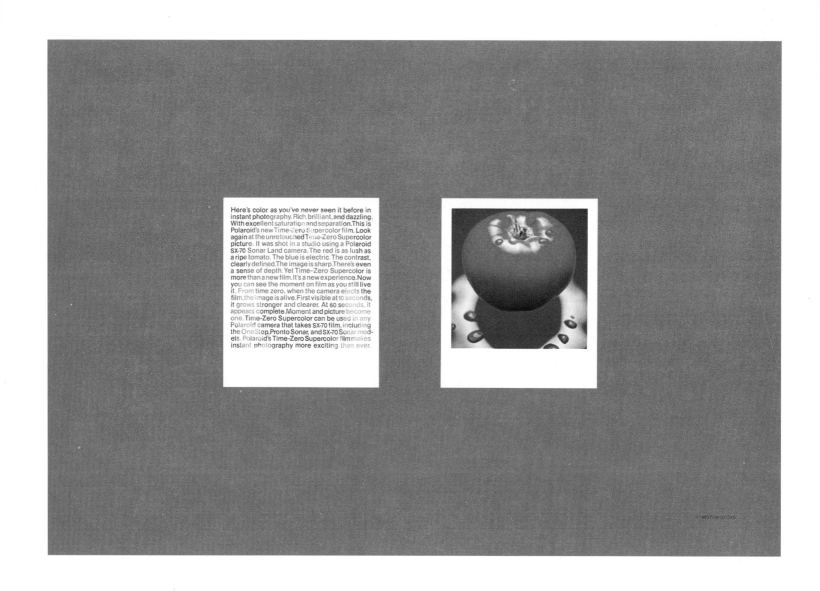

"I wouldn't hesitate for a second to choose the plain-looking ad that is alive and vital and meaningful over the ad that is beautiful but dumb."

"Today's smartest advertising style is tomorrow's corn."

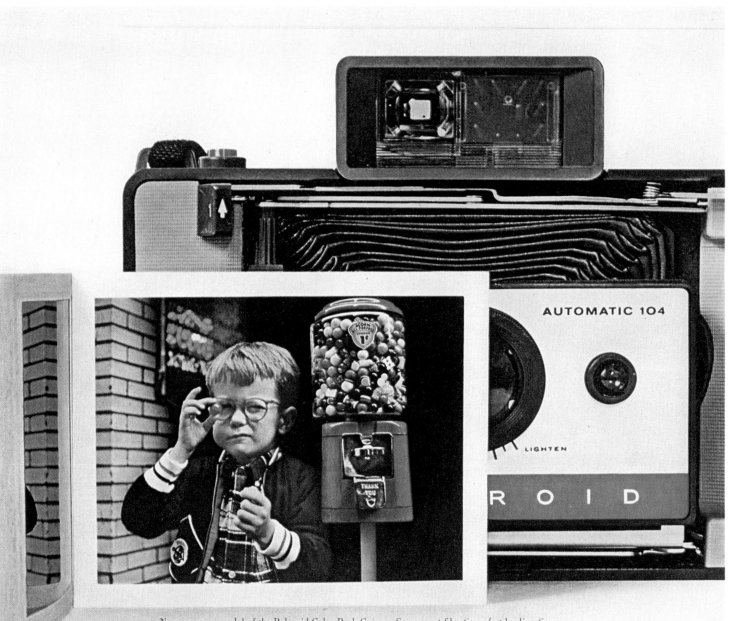

New economy model of the Polaroid Color Pack Camera. Same great film. Same fast loading. Same big color prints in 60 seconds (black and white in 10). Yet it's half the price of the original model!

60 seconds. Under $60.

"POLAROID"®

Polaroid "Zoo"

1 Music

2 Music

3 Music

4 Music

5 Music

6 If you're not taking color pictures with the new Polaroid Color-Pak Camera, there's something left out of your life.

Polaroid "Visit to Grandpa"

1   I used to think I could stop the earth, and hold time in my hands.

2   But I watched it as it raced on by me, heading for tomorrow.

3   So when this day is over, and the sun leaves the sky,

4   Let me see all the memories while they're clear in my eye.

5   Let me reach out and touch all the faces and places that I love so much.

6   Especially the people that I love so much.

Polaroid SX-70 "Laurence Olivier"

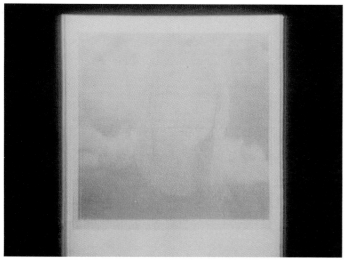

1 Now there's a radically new photographic system that hands you a picture less than two seconds after you take it.

2 The minutes as the image blooms, you realize you've never before seen a photograph so startlingly real.

3 This is what makes it possible. The new SX-70.

4 Ready to propel picture after picture into your hand just as quickly as you can touch the electric button.

5 Minutes later, you'll have a finished photograph of such dazzling beauty that you'll feel you're looking at the world for the first time.

6 The new SX-70 Land Camera. From Polaroid.

Polaroid "Garner and Hartley"

1   Garner: Polaroid's One-Step is the world's simplest camera. Even a woman could use it. Hartley: How's that again? Garner: I thought that would get her attention.

2   Hartley: I could have a thousand women here in half an hour . . . All marching with big signs . . .

3   Garner: You never focus, just point it and press the button.

4   Garner: The sharp clear color develops in minutes. You're beautiful when you're angry.

5   Hartley: You had a nice career there for a while.

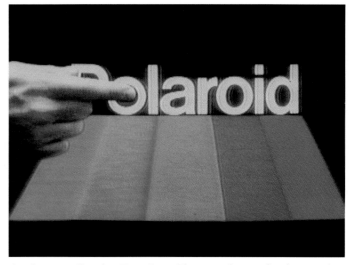

6   Garner: Get the One-Step. This may be my final appeal.

American
Airlines

A very happy by-product of Doyle Dane Bernbach's advertising for El Al Israel Airlines was that it attracted the attention of a somewhat larger client: American Airlines.

As an experiment, Bill pinned dozens of competitive airlines' ads to his wall, covered up the names and logotypes, and discovered (not too surprisingly) that they were pretty much interchangeable—including American's.

For precisely the same reasons that clear, truthful, believable corporate personalities were created for Ohrbach's, for El Al, for Levy's, for Volkswagen, for Polaroid, the agency set about creating such a personality for American Airlines.

It began with a series of cartoon drawings (by themselves significantly different from the graphics used by other airlines) that touched on topics dear to the business traveler, American's bread-and-butter customer.

"People keep stealing our stewardesses," "Any time you want to leave your wife is all right with us," "If the thought of a trip gives you a headache," and "You're not Alice" established a tone of service and quality based on truth. That was the backbone of American Airlines' advertising for more than two decades.

For example, when American tried to persuade business travelers to upgrade to first class, there were no photographs of grinning cabin attendants serving up champagne and caviar. Instead, ads such as "Why generals have always had a tent of their own" and "When Disraeli closed his door, England made history" appeared.

Bill understood that the rationale of privacy and of useful thinking time was more powerful than the limitless booze and fancy food that were forthcoming anyway. The advertising turned first-class travel from a suspicious indulgence into a practical necessity for the professional traveler.

This attitude of professionalism was not lost on the vacation travelers, many of whom were business travelers on holiday. But the strength of the image was enough to allow posters such as "Take one home to Mother" and "Best restaurant between New York and L.A." to reach out to new audiences. And to allow ads such as "Why should you wait longer for your luggage than Henry Fonda does?," "American Airlines doesn't care what your luggage weighs," and "Bring the kiddies for ⅔ off" to enhance American's personality rather than to chip away at it.

The potent image of American Airlines was probably expressed best in DDB's "Doing what we do best" campaign, a comprehensive effort that incorporated a stirring musical theme and emotionally charged messages with basic "origin and destination" information.

DDB and American Airlines literally parted ways in 1981, when American Airlines moved its corporate headquarters to Dallas.

The musical echo of the "Doing what we do best" campaign, however, still reverberates.

"You're not Alice."

No, that isn't Alice.

Alice isn't with us anymore.

And we understand the "regulars" on her flight aren't very happy about it.

After you flew with Alice once, she remembered your face the next time.

And your *name* the next time.

And that you liked your coffee with saccharin after *that*.

And what happened to Alice?

Well, if you must know, one of you married her.

In fact, one or another of you has married practically every stewardess we've ever had.

(It's got to the point now where we can't keep girls more than 2 years.)

So don't look at us that way if you miss Alice or Doreen or Nora.

You can't go on removing these girls from the premises and still expect to find them on the airplane.

American Airlines

Any time you want to leave your wife is all right with us.

The opportunity presents itself every two hours—if you're leaving her for Los Angeles. (Plus a late evening flight, too.)

Five of the seven flights offer Astrovision —the choice of a movie, or classical and popular music in stereo. These are the 10 a.m., and the 2, 4, 6, and 8 p.m. flights. (Incidentally, the 2 p.m. flight leaves from Newark Airport.)

You can make reservations (First Class and Royal Coachman) through your travel agent or call us direct. And you can charge the fare on your American Express card.

One thing more—and your wife might like this—we've got every-two-hour service coming back, too.

American Airlines: every 2 hours to Los Angeles

10 am

12 noon

2 pm

4 pm

6 pm

8 pm

11:15 pm

People keep stealing our stewardesses.

Within 2 years, most of our stewardesses will leave us for other men.

This isn't surprising. A girl who can smile for 5½ hours is hard to find.

Not to mention a wife who can remember what 124 people want for dinner. (And tell you all about meteorology and jets, if that's what you're looking for in a woman.)

But these things aren't what brought on our problem. It's the kind of girl we hire. Being beautiful isn't enough. We don't mean it isn't important. We just mean it isn't enough.

So if there's one thing we look for, it's girls who like people.

And you can't do that and then tell them not to like people too much.

All you can do is put a new wing on your stewardess college to keep up with the demand.

American Airlines

Bring the kiddies for ²⁄₃ off.

If he's Little Billy to you, he's Little Billy to us and you can bring him along for next to nothing.

In our book, "little" means under 22. (You have to grow up *sometime*.)

The only string is that your wife go along, too—and we'll take ⅓ off her fare. (If only one parent goes, Billy gets the ⅓ off and his brothers get the ²⁄₃ off.) So one out of three of you flies for nothing.

Now, the fares we're talking about are already just about the lowest jet fares we have—our Royal Coachman seats.

But we might point out that Royal Coachman includes a movie on Astro-vision, beverages, lunch or dinner and any number of other little services. We never, never call Royal Coachman the "cheap seats."

These fares are good Monday noon to Friday noon, but please don't wait. (When Billy's 22, the deal's off.)

American Airlines

Why generals have always had a tent of their own.

Thoughts on first class travel—a series by American Airlines.

Gen."Stonewall" Jackson, hero of Chancellorsville.

It is not because rank hath its privileges. The reason is much simpler.

The man who's supposed to be thinking about the battle needs a place to do it in.

It's the same with the extra service that a general gets. The idea is to free him from the usual annoyances so he can concentrate on getting the war won.

These are also the reasons a man with business on his mind flies first class.

The privacy, the roominess, the comfort and the over-all atmosphere ease the burden of travel for men under pressure.

Business travellers have been the mainstay of our company for some 25 years now. Fully 86% of all air trips are strictly for business. And our first class service emerged as the result of just this.

It was not designed for the so-called carriage trade, and it is not an investment in luxury.

It's an investment in the man who gets off the plane.

If you would like to know more about the habits and patterns of the business traveller, please write to: Director, Bureau of Travel Analysis, American Airlines, Inc., 633 Third Ave., New York 17, N.Y.

Loosen your seat belt.

First Class dinner service.

AMERICAN AIRLINES TO NEW YORK

"Forget words like 'hard sell' and 'soft sell.' That will only confuse you. Just be sure your advertising is saying something with substance, something that will inform and serve the consumer, and be sure you're saying it like it's never been said before."

"A great campaign will make a bad product fail faster. It will get more people to know it's bad."

Best place to eat between here and N.Y.

"If you stand for something, you will always find some people for you and some against you. If you stand for nothing, you will find nobody against you, and nobody *for you*."

"Can you really judge an idea from a storyboard? How do you storyboard a smile?"

American Airlines "Lyric"

1   I love flying far and wide to see the land I love,

2   Climb to find the blue horizon, the sun and sky above.

3   It's my flight and I know it's right and I just smile inside.

4   From the sunrise in the east, to the sunset in the west,

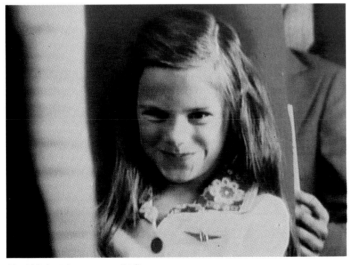

5   We're American Airlines,

6   Doing what we do best . . .

Clairol

t's not unusual for an ad agency to get assignments for products that are either 1) no place or 2) going no place. Clairol gave DDB one of each.

Clairol assigned Nice 'n Easy to DDB in 1969 because business was bad and getting worse.

The early signs of women's liberation were there—if you knew where to look and how to interpret what you found. Research—everyone's research—correctly pointed out that women wanted to look "natural." And advertising—everyone's advertising—incorrectly claimed "Look natural with Brand X." Incorrectly, because when competing advertisers all make the same claim, the consumer doesn't know whom to believe and ends up believing no one.

DDB went beyond all this and captured the essence of what women were feeling: It was OK to be yourself, to be free, to do what you want to do, wear what you want to wear.

The advertising showed young women expressing these feelings and concluded with a line saying, "It lets me be me." Which meant, "You're really terrific, and we'll help you make the most of it."

Even then many TV ads were subjected to tests that measure the percentage of people who remember a commercial, what they remember about it, their attitudes toward it, whether or not they intend to buy the product, etc. Despite the appalling distinction of achieving some of the lowest scores ever recorded for any commercials, the "It lets me be me" campaign restored Nice 'n Easy to its number one position in the market, where it remains today.

The contradiction between poor test scores and success in the marketplace reinforced Bill's unshakable skepticism about predictive research. "We are so busy measuring public opinion, we forget that we can mold it" expresses his feelings in printable form.

The second product, Final Net, had been sold in small quantities by beauty salons before Clairol bought it in 1972.

It was an excellent product that hadn't enjoyed national advertising or distribution or awareness.

The highly advertised hair sprays were then running campaigns in which women were run through car washes, gale-force winds, and other hardships to show the holding power of their products.

DDB's Final Net campaign showed women doing somewhat more normal things, such as teaching school, going to a dance, being a TV newscaster. In every case, the star of the commercial either dozed off or fell completely asleep, with her hair looking wonderful. The summary line of the campaign was "She conked out, but her hair held up. Final Net lasts longer than you do." There was also a claim that stated, "Final Net lasts 3 times longer than the leading hair spray." In a relatively short time, the claim had to be abandoned because Final Net itself became the leading hair spray.

If you have to lose a claim on legal grounds, that's surely the way.

Put your hand over the gray half and see how much younger I look.

It lets me be me.

In hair color, as in make-up, clothes, love, work…a woman wants to be herself. Not somebody else's idea of what she is, or should be.

That's what women like about Nice 'n Easy. Whether you want to color or conceal, to change a little or a lot, Nice 'n Easy assures you of beautiful coverage, healthy-looking hair and honest color that becomes part of you.

No wonder, now more than ever, it sells the most.

"To succeed, an ad (or a person or product, for that matter) must establish its own unique personality, or it will never be noticed."

"Logic and overanalysis can immobilize and sterilize an idea. It's like love—the more you analyze it, the faster it disappears."

Clairol / 101

It lets me be me.*

In hair color, as in make-up, clothes, love, work...a woman wants to be herself. Not somebody else's idea of what she is, or should be. That's what women like about Nice'n Easy.® Whether you want to color or conceal, to change a little or a lot, Nice'n Easy assures you of beautiful coverage, healthy-looking hair and honest color that becomes part of you.

No wonder, now more than ever, it sells the most. Nice'n Easy. From Clairol.

Nice'n Easy

"An important idea not communicated persuasively
is like having no idea at all."

Colombian Coffee

f you're feeling up to a great challenge, try selling something that nobody can buy.

Doyle Dane Bernbach was and did.

The assignment was from the Federation of Coffee Growers of Colombia: "Get the public to look for and buy those brands of coffee with Colombian coffee in the blend."

Easy. Just get people to invest their precious time reading coffee cans.

To do this, DDB invented a character named Juan Valdez, who typifies all of the Colombian coffee growers. Juan Valdez, as we all know, picks his coffee beans one at a time, providing us with "the richest coffee in the world."

The idea behind the campaign was to suggest to coffee roasters that they would sell more coffee if they added Colombian coffee to their blends and labeled their packages to say so. The advertising in turn would provide a ready market.

This unlikely scenario has actually been working for nearly a quarter of a century. In fact, there are now dozens of brands of 100 percent Colombian coffee and a problem of supply rather than demand.

As the actors who portrayed Juan Valdez have aged, DDB has hired more youthful ones who continue to pick their beans "Juan by Juan."

Juan Valdez, coffee planter, proudly shows the entire yield of one tree.

Somebody called the region where Juan Valdez lives "fit only for eagles and mules."

But it is a paradise for coffee growing, 5,000 feet up in the Colombian Andes, where the soil is rich and the air moist.

Juan could let his coffee trees stand in the burning sun. But, like all the men who grow Colombian coffee, he plants tall trees to shade them (and bring out a remarkable flavor). He stubbornly picks the beans one by one, to be sure he takes only the ripe ones. The result, only one pound of coffee from each tree.

But it has more character than any coffee in the world. Colombian coffee is invariably the dominant flavor in good brands (the more Colombian coffee, the better the blend).

Coffee of Colombia

How to pick a pound of Colombian coffee off this page.

(1) Get a huge air blower and put in the beans. The heavy ones will fall. The light ones stay aloft and will be carried away. Keep only the heavy ones. They have more character.

(2) Pick only the evenly colored, firm beans. None with speckles. No black ones. This is part of the secret of Colombian coffee's smooth, even taste. Really extraordinary.

(3) Pay no attention to the *size* of the beans. It is weight and color that count. Colombians are so finicky about grading coffee, many of the beans you see here will never be shipped.

(4) Now the beans are ready for roasting. Colombian coffee is invariably the dominant flavor in good coffee brands. (Brew your coffee good and rich. It takes an honest brew to do coffee justice.)

Fame has its price.

"Doctor, it's gotten to the point where people are constantly asking for my autograph. I can't even eat my chorizos in peace."

These words recently came from the fatigued form of Juan Valdez.® Along with his partner he's starting to feel the pressure of success.

The cause of it all, of course, is their huge television exposure for Colombian Coffee. In fact this year alone, Juan and his friend will be seen almost 2 billion times in American living rooms.

Frankly they've proven to be successful spokesmen. A recent survey indicates that most Americans now believe that Colombian Coffee is the best in the world. Which, unfortunately for Juan, makes him even more popular.

What this means to you is that if you're not offering a 100% Colombian Coffee brand, it's time to start. Every day you delay you're losing potential profits.

And if you let that happen you'll end up like Juan. Spilling the beans to a psychiatrist. The National Federation of Coffee Growers of Colombia, 140 East 57th Street, New York, N.Y. 10022

100% Colombian Coffee

"Nobody counts the number of ads you run; they just remember the impression you make."

Colombia Coffee "Rain"

1 In Colombia, South America, we live high in the Andes, close to the clouds.

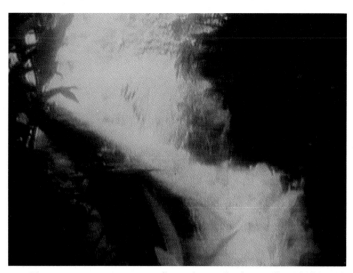

2 Clear mountain waters flow through the coffee fields of Juan Valdez and enrich the earth.

3 The coffee beans grow delicious with flavor as they ripen slowly in the moist mountain air.

4 Juan and his son even wash the beans in the fresh mountain water to keep the flavor pure.

5 To grow coffee this good, you need the Colombian rain.

6 But to make it, all you need is 100 percent Colombian coffee.

Porsche

A Porsche isn't "sold" in the normal sense of selling. "Heaven" isn't sold in the normal sense either, but there are an awful lot of temptations, distractions, and pitfalls along the way in both cases.

Many times advertising has to provide an emotional reason for someone to buy a product: good looks, good health, love, money, and so on.

Porsche provides its own emotional reasons. DDB always felt that by supplying enough tantalizing facts and information, it could both inform the public and bring some of those emotional reasons to the boiling point.

It was also crucial to keep reassuring current Porsche owners about the wisdom of their purchase, since the majority of new Porsches are sold to owners of older Porsches.

With photographs more jewel-like than car-like, with explosive layouts, and with lengthy, informative copy, growing numbers of people felt that they not only wanted a Porsche but that they *needed* one.

Just as a great painting is more than canvas and paints, there are some things that go beyond the sum of their parts.

The Porsche Targa is such an object.

It is a piece of machinery whose purpose far exceeds transporting you from one point to another. The Targa's goal is to afford the ultimate driving experience. In performance, in engineering, in comfort.

The Targa has come amazingly close to that goal: each year, with subtle improvements, a bit more.

First, consider its superbly thought-out features. It has a built-in roll bar, and a huge fixed rear window. To give the car the practicality of a hard-top coupe. And you the exhila-rating experience of a roadster.

It has an aerodynamic shape, to protect you from wind blast. And a rear-engine design that has been steadily improved upon for

"That's IT"

25 years.

All controls are meticu-lously engineered to be functional and logically accessible.

Yet it is the total effect of these innovations that impresses.

With the removable top stored in the trunk, cushioned in luxurious bucket seats, you ride in "Belle Epoque" comfort.

But the grandest feature of the Targa is the experience of driving it.

The handling is quick, correct, precise, because of Porsche's legendary engineering. Putting the driver and car in perfect collaboration. It is almost as if you just "think" where you want the car to go.

The Targa is available in all three 911 models: 911T, 911E, and 911S.

But be warned.

It is very difficult to be humble about owning any Porsche. And if it's a Targa, that's IT.

"The magic is in the product."

"It's that creative spark that I'm so jealous of for our agency and that I'm so desperately fearful of losing. I don't want academicians. I don't want scientists. I don't want people who do the right things. *I want people who do inspiring things.*"

In a race there are two things you can count on. The unexpected and the unpredictable. So the car must respond with an almost animal quickness and sureness.

Speed alone is not enough. Every part of the car must possess the utmost in reliability. For Porsche, racing is the ultimate test of that.

We use the classic courses and tracks of the world as our research laboratories. They are the proving and improving grounds for established ideas. And the headwaters of inspiration for new ones.

It is not incidental that we have been the world's champions for the last 3 years in a row.

The more we race, the more features we prove. And only when something has passed the test of the track does it ever show up on a car for the street.

Everything we've learned goes into the Mid-Engine Porsche 914 and the Porsche 911.

At Porsche we do not race to make a name; we race to build a car.

For dealer information call (free) 800-553-9550. In Iowa (collect) 319-242-1327.

"Racing is the ultimate test." Dr. Ferry Porsche

"It is ironic that the very thing that is most suspected by business, that intangible thing called artistry, turns out to be the most practical tool available to it. For it is only an original talent that can vie with all the shocking news events and violence in the world for the attention of the consumer."

"Maybe we're getting bogged down in too much detail.
Maybe our advertising ideas are being ground up in that
multilevel American efficiency machine."

"The real giants have always been poets, men who jumped from facts into the realm of imagination and ideas."

"I warn you against believing that advertising is a science."

Porsche 928S

Consumer Orientation No. 20 in a Series of Technical Papers

Subject: Introduction of the 928S. New Power. New Performance. New Parameters of Comfort and Luxury in Porsche's Finest.

At Porsche, our philosophy is to design, test, produce, and constantly improve. The new 928S embodies this tradition and is the proud successor to the 928. Consider its aluminum-alloy V-8 engine. Displacement has been increased to 4.7 liters. And output has been raised to 234 hp. On the track, with manual transmission, the 928S accelerates from 0 to 50 mph in 5.2 seconds. And it has a maximum speed of 146 mph. The 928S' transaxle design produces balanced front-to-rear weight for improved cornering and balanced braking. And it creates a high polar moment of inertia for increased directional control. The 928S' unique Weissach rear axle optimizes rear-wheel alignment during deceleration or braking and while cornering. A kinematic effect changes toe-out to toe-in in no more than 0.2 seconds to control oversteer. The 928S' aerodynamic design includes integral front and rear spoilers to reduce lift and improve road holding. Inside, standard equipment includes: An adjustable-tilt steering column and instrument cluster. Power steering. Power disc brakes. A power driver's seat. And a choice of 5-speed manual or new 4-speed automatic transmission. Priced at $43,000; the new 928S is Porsche's finest. For your dealer, call toll-free: (800) 447-4700. In Illinois, (800) 322-4400.

PORSCHE + AUDI NOTHING EVEN COMES CLOSE

*Manufacturer's suggested retail price. Title, taxes, transportation, registration and dealer delivery charges additional. © 1982 Porsche Audi.

"The truth isn't the truth until people believe you; and they can't believe you if they don't know what you're saying; and they can't know what you're saying if they don't listen to you; and they won't listen to you if you're not interesting. And you won't be interesting unless you say things freshly, originally, imaginatively."

"We are so busy measuring public opinion that we forget we can mold it. We are so busy listening to statistics we forget we can create them."

"You cannot sell a man who isn't listening."

Alka-Seltzer

Two of the best-known and certainly the most humorous and telling Alka-Seltzer commercials were created by Doyle Dane Bernbach.

"Mamma mia" and "Poached oysters" are enduring examples of humor at its relevant best. Every word and every action in both of these commercials point to Alka-Seltzer for relief from indigestion.

At one meeting, DDB was asked to do a catchall commercial for Alka-Seltzer. "What else is it good for besides indigestion?" Bill asked.

"Headaches, hangovers, depression, *everything*" was the answer. "Good," Bill shot back, "next time I have everything, I'll take some."

That put an end to that argument, but another argument about humor in analgesic advertising still continues.

Despite the popularity of the commercials, sales of Alka-Seltzer began to drop. Somehow this slump was attributed to the fact that the commercials were funny.

DDB maintained that the introduction of Alka-Seltzer Plus, a cold remedy, was an error because the new name implied a superior version of Alka-Seltzer without any indication of what the new product was really all about. The fear was that the new product would cannibalize the old. And it did.

Alka-Seltzer Plus, being new and sounding improved (and backed by DDB advertising), sold quite a lot of product. The basic Alka-Seltzer sales indeed dropped, as DDB predicted. In the aggregate, however, Alka-Seltzer and Alka-Seltzer Plus together had a considerably greater share of the market than Alka-Seltzer had had alone.

It's a strain to believe that anyone could conclude from this that humorous advertising caused a drop in sales, but that's exactly the conclusion that was reached.

DDB continued to believe that commercials like "Mamma mia" —which has the distinction of having been named the "World's Best Television Commercial" at the International Broadcasting Awards in 1980 and which everyone, including the "experts," felt was a masterpiece at the time—only helped Alka-Seltzer's cause.

1   Mamma Mia, thats'a some specie . . .
Cut. That's *spicy* meatball.

2   Take twenty-eight. Mamma Mia, that's a spicy meat-
ball . . . Cut.
What's wrong with that?
Wrong accent.

3   Ugh, hot.
Cut.

4   Meesy, micy . . .
Cut. Take fifty-nine.

5   (VO) Sometimes you eat more than you should and when
it's spicy besides, Mamma Mia, do you need Alka-Seltzer.
Alka-Seltzer can help unstuff you, relieve the acid indigestion,
and help make you your old self again.

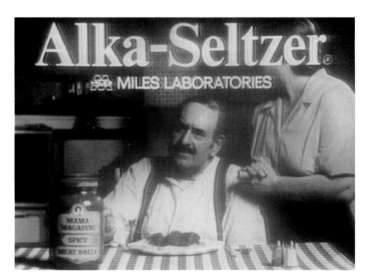

6   Mamma Mia, that's a spicy meatball . . .
Cut. Let's break for lunch.

Alka-Seltzer "Poached Oyster"

1 Our first home-cooked meal. I'm glad you liked it, dear.

2 I'll say. I've never seen a dumpling that big. I'm sorry I couldn't finish the whole dumpling. I had to throw it out."

3 I froze it! It wasn't on the heavy side, was it?"

4 Let's see, what would you like tomorrow night? Stuffed crab surprise . . . creamed duck delight. . . . Is it beginning to rain, dear?

5 . . . marshmallow meat balls . . . sweet and sour snails, yum! Poached oysters . . .

6 What love doesn't conquer, Alka-Seltzer will.

Utica Club,
Rheingold,
Stroh's

A "brand personality" is perhaps more important in beer advertising than in any other.

Yet it takes a fine eye and a fine ear to distinguish the advertising of one major brand of beer from another. While many beer drinkers are able to do so, the remarkably similar advertising doesn't make it easy for them.

In the early sixties, DDB did the advertising for an upstate New York beer called Utica Club. The "brand personality" for Utica Club very nearly presented itself in a comment made by Mr. Walter J. Matt, the brewery owner.

"I don't know what to tell you," said Mr. Matt with some bitterness. "We have one of the great breweries in America. We have the best malt, the best hops, we have the latest equipment that my father brought over from Germany. But sometimes I wonder if it pays to make beer this way. People want a gimmick."

That was the personality, and that was the headline: "I sometimes wonder if it pays to make beer this way."

It wasn't slick. It broke the rules about not scolding your customers. It didn't say, "Buy me, I'm best." It was an angry man talking, and because he was angry and human, people believed him.

The ad bore his signature, and literally thousands of people wrote to Mr. Matt personally, saying, "Please don't go out of business. America needs honest businessmen like you."

The Utica Club print campaign—unslick as it could be, together with a television campaign featuring Schultz and Dooley, an engaging pair of animated beer mugs—sent sales through the roof of the brewery. Mr. Matt was totally convinced that he had written the advertising himself, and, in a way, he had. The "brand personality" and his own personality were one and the same.

As a result of the Utica Club success, DDB came to the attention of Rheingold, at the time the brewers of the largest-selling beer in New York City.

New York City, the melting pot, is almost entirely composed of a huge variety of ethnic groups—Irish, Jewish, Italian, Puerto Rican, black, Greek, Chinese, Polish. The great temptation in developing a "brand personality" was to say in the advertising that at least one thing that all these peoples had in common was their brand of beer—Rheingold. That's what DDB did.

Beautifully shot television commercials showed various ethnic holidays and celebrations, all accompanied by Rheingold beer. And the copy asked, "Why do more Chinese-Americans [for example] drink Rheingold than any other beer? We don't know. But we must be doing something right."

It was truthful. It was certainly human. It was different. But no one anticipated hate. Maybe nice people don't think about hate. But it was there, and it was vituperative. Unprintable letters and serious threats came by the dozens. "I won't drink the same beer as those *!?*'s.'' It was a colossal misjudgment. The pot needed a lot more melting. It probably still does.

The Stroh Brewery in Detroit either didn't know or didn't care about Rheingold. They did care about selling Stroh's, and DDB got the assignment in 1968.

Stroh's Beer is fire-brewed, an expensive and time-consuming process that, in America, is unique to Stroh's. The agency felt that a family-owned brewery, still committed to a time-honored method of making beer, was the essence of a Stroh ''brand personality.'' With language that promised a product that came ''from one beer lover to another'' and distinctive executions that are still acknowledged to be the models of the business, DDB helped Stroh grow from the twelfth largest to the third largest brewery in the country.

Any mug can taste the difference

—between a beer that's brewed from whole grain and beers made from syrups or concentrates. Between a beer that's been aged for months and beers turned out in weeks. Between real foam and artificial bubbles. Between a beer that's still made by an old-fashioned brewmaster and beers made by scientists. Try a bottle of Utica Club beer tonight and taste the difference yourself. The West End Brewing Company of Utica, N.Y. **Utica Club**

Our beer is 50 years behind the times
(and we're proud of it)

"No matter how skillful you are, you can't invent a product advantage that doesn't exist. And if you do, and it's just a gimmick, it's going to fall apart anyway."

Rheingold "Italian Version"

1 (VO) An Italian wedding is a warm affair.

2 Much *tarantella* and much affection.

3 The beer that's often used to cool things off is Rheingold Extra Dry.

4 In fact, in New York City, where there are more Italians than in all of Venice, more people drink Rheingold than any other beer.

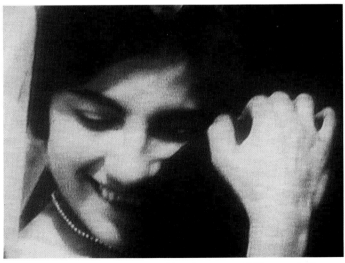

5 Why do Italian Americans like the taste of Rheingold?

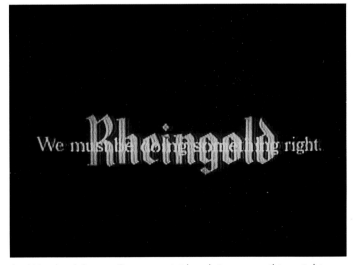

6 We don't know. But we must be doing something right.

"Execution becomes content in a work of genius."

"You can say the right thing about a product and nobody will listen. You've got to say it in such a way that people will feel it in their gut. Because if they don't feel it, nothing will happen."

Stroh's "Lost Patrol"

1   All right men, take a break.

2   Ah, Yank, what about some of that Stroh's beer what you've been talking about?

3   Aah, marvelous.

4   Save some of that for the rest of us, Alfie.

6   Pick it up, mate. We don't want the blokes to know we've been here.

From one beer lover to another.
THE STROH BREWERY COMPANY, DETROIT, MICHIGAN 48226

Jamaica

Without doubt, DDB's print advertising for Jamaica was the most beautiful and, at the same time, probably the most informative travel advertising ever done.

On television, it was also the *first* travel advertising ever done. The technique of compressing an entire vacation into a sixty-second (and later thirty-second) mini-travelogue was totally new as well. Tourism soared.

Today travel advertising is commonplace on television, and it would be fair to say that all of it, print and TV, carries the echo of Jamaica.

JAMAICA

Ella Mae and Lascelles Ormsby, married January 9, St. James Anglican Church, Burnam Wood. They honeymooned in Jamaica.

The bride carried a bouquet of jasmine.

(But from her garden, not a florist.)

The groom wore a white flower in his hatband.

(Instead of his buttonhole.)

150 guests came in ruffled, brocaded and tulle-y yellows, pinks, blues. And black suits.

(Like at weddings anywhere.)

Leaving church, the couple walked under palm bowers.

(Instead of ducking rice.)

At the reception, they were toasted with rum, then feasted on curried goat, green banana, and hard dough bread, which is chewy like pumpernickel, but white.

(No champagne, no chicken, no chopped liver.)

Instead of *sleeping* on the wedding cake that night, everyone *bet* on it that afternoon. This is how we give gifts of money. We bet on whether the draped wedding cake should be uncovered or not, putting the money in "betting" saucers.

(Instead of envelopes.)

In the evening, dancing. The ska. The reggae. The quadrille.

(Our jerk, lindy, waltz.)

Then the happy pair went on their honeymoon. They stepped inside their little Jamaican house.

(No plans for sailing, snorkeling, skin-diving, water-skiing, golfing, or going nightclubbing.)

That's marriage, Jamaican-style.

Not radically unlike yours.

Except—we never have to come home from our Jamaican honeymoons.

For all about the kind you come home from, see your local travel agent or Jamaica Tourist Board in New York, Chicago, Los Angeles, San Francisco, Miami, Toronto, Montreal.

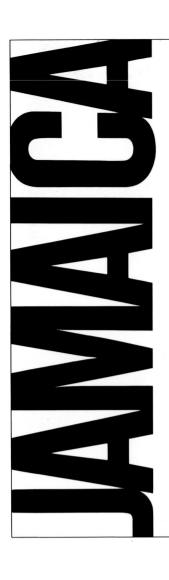

JAMAICA

Jamaica may be the
only country in the world
where you can
dance under the stars
to sweet music.
And the strains of
cockadoodledoo.

You're cheek-to-cheeking.
(Or having a steak. Or moon-watching. Or even smooching.)
And suddenly it will dawn on you. Faintly, faraway, maybe. But always ridiculously in the air.
Morning, noon, night.
Cockadoodledoooooooooooo.
Crowing is Jamaica's National Sound.
Runners-up: the beat of our music (*oomska, oomska*). And our *off*beat English (we eat *coocoombers*, wash with *Palm-a-leaf* soap, see Bette Davis *flims*).
We also have National Smells. Sugary air (anywhere cane is cut). Hot-peppered air (anywhere we cook). And our night air (so thick with warm fragrances you could lick it).
Our National Taste is rum. Up to 200 proof. (Called "Kill Daddy.") Followed by inflammatory curried goat and calming rice 'n' peas.
Our National Thing to See is probably *us*. We blend Europe, China and Africa in our faces. We mix colors like purple, cerise and chartreuse in our clothes.
Our National Touch Thing?
Maybe the cushion-y feel of our sea.
Or the tender flutter of a hummingbird as it lights on your finger at Miss Salmon's.
Or our Dorothy McNab silks—light, fragile, barely touching as they blow about you, gossamer, slithery, quivery. Sigh.
For more of our mouth-watering, skin-tingling, sweet-smelling, eye-catching, cockadoodling country, see your local travel agent or Jamaica Tourist Board in New York, San Francisco, Chicago, Miami, Los Angeles, Toronto, Montreal.
© JAMAICA TOURIST BOARD

"Finding out what to say is the beginning of the communication process. How you say it makes people look and listen and believe. And if you are not successful at that you have wasted all the work and intelligence and skill that went into discovering what you should say."

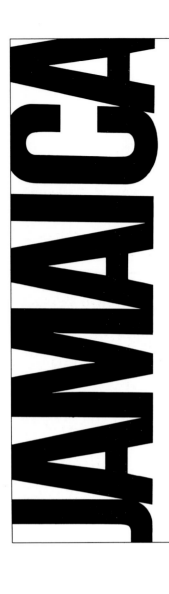

People become Jamaica fans
because of the
beautiful sun, sea,
beaches, flowers, hotels.
And other reasons.

Women, especially women of
Montego Bay, have always helped
make our land desirable.

A woman, *Maybelle Ewen,*
opened the first Mo'bay hotel
(Casablanca) in 1924.

Today there are 52 (including
Miranda Hill and Good *Hope*) with
prized rooms for 6087 pleasure-
loving people.

Many are managed by women.

Stephanie Chin. Austrian-born
doyenne of picturesque Richmond
Hill Inn, will whip you up weiner
schnitzel. Personally.

Irene Holloway pampers scuba-
divers at Chalet Caribe.

American *Mrs. Gold* mistresses a
very Jamaican Inn (Sign).

Jamaican *Miss dePass* (Verney
House) specializes in English teas.

Meet our famous ghost, *Annie
Palmer,* at sumptuous Rose Hall.

Raft down a river called *Martha
Brae.*

Drink a liqueur named *Rumona.*

It's women who higgle (sell
goods) and haggle (haggle) at huge
Coronation Market.

Women are police, preachers,
barkeeps.

Women are the limberest limbo
dancers.

The woman at right?

Sintra Berrington, a homebody
who cooks curries and suns at
Doctors Cave Beach.

And takes shorthand, too.

For more of sybaritic Mo'bay
(*and* pastoral Ocho Rios, cultural
Kingston, peaceful Port Antonio),
see a travel agent or Jamaica Tourist
Board in New York, Chicago, San
Francisco, Los Angeles, Washing-
ton, D.C., Miami, Detroit, Toronto,
Montreal. © 1972 JAMAICA TOURIST BOARD.

"Because an appeal makes logical sense is no guarantee
that it will work."

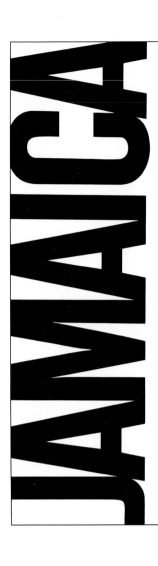

What makes young
Elcylin Whyte feel so pleased?
Her jaunty hat?
Her pretty dress?
The sunshine day?
You?

We're like this, we Jamaicans: we don't go around always acting smily and jovial. But we *re*-act. Easily.

Elcylin is being Jamaican. Someone is snapping her picture. And smiling. So she's smiling back. (You can almost see a picture of *him*.)

That's our way.

Let us tell you more about the kind of people we are.

We're good listeners. In conversation, we zero in on *you*. And maybe that's what's called our "charm."

But we're rabid talkers, too. "We talk like rivers flow." Which may be why a lot of us are lawyers and preachers. And why every cabbie is a Tour Conductor.

We're religious (more than 400 sects, including tambourine revival).

We're definitely matriarchal. Mothers are our pillars. And our Nanny Loving Care is famed.

We're quite artful. In our dress (uncommon color pairings). And paintings (*everyone* dabbles, even with house enamel). And in the way we often paint our *houses* (with fantasy).

We move well. "Man, we dance from top to bottom. The neck is involved, the nose, the ears, the toes are involved."

We are more lean than fat. Proud and courteous.

And, mostly, we're un-neurotic. (Maybe we're talked out.) "There are a few psychiatrists here but I don't think they do much business."

For *all* about Coming to Know Us, see a travel agent or Jamaica Tourist Board in New York, Los Angeles, Chicago, Miami, Detroit, San Francisco, Toronto, Montreal.

© 1970 JAMAICA TOURIST BOARD

"Dullness won't sell your product, but neither will
    irrelevant brilliance."

"An idea can turn to dust or magic, depending
on the talent that rubs against it."

Jamaica "Contrasts"

1 It has mountains.

2 It's obvious.

3 It's exciting.

4 It's cool.

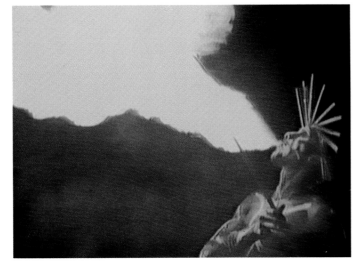

5 It's wild.

6 That's Jamaica.

"There are two attitudes you can wear: that of cold arithmetic or that of warm human persuasion. I will urge the latter on you. For there is evidence that in the field of communications, the more intellectual you grow, the more you lose the great intuitive skills that make for the greatest persuasion—the things that really touch and move people."

"There is practically nothing that is not capable of boring us."

Life Cereal

"Mikey" was only one commercial.

And not much of one, if you go by test scores. The scores were dismal, and the commercial was aired with considerable reluctance.

Yet, overnight "Mikey" himself became a national hero, "Mikey likes it!" became part of the American language, and carloads of Life cereal vanished into the mouths of unsuspecting kids, who didn't know that it was good for them.

The idea of having a small child, too innocent to know that "if it's good for me, it must taste awful," cheerfully slurp up a bowl of Life cereal simply because he liked it certainly is a good concept.

But the execution itself—the genuineness of the casting (yes, they really *were* brothers) and the brilliant direction are what made that one commercial so popular for so long.

There are some who believe that once a selling proposition is arrived at, the job is essentially done.

There are also some who believe that the earth is flat.

"However much we would like advertising to be a science
—because life would be simpler that way—the fact is that
it is not. It is a subtle, ever-changing art, defying
formulization, flowering on freshness, and withering on
imitation; where what was effective one day, for that very
reason will not be effective the next, because
it has lost the maximum impact of originality."

Life Cereal "Mikey"

1 What's this stuff?
Some cereal. It's supposed to be good for you.

2 Did you try it?
I'm not gonna try it. You try it.

3 Let's get Mikey.

4 He won't eat it. He hates everything.

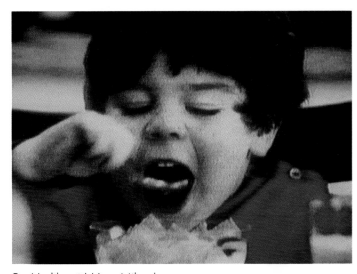

5 He likes it! Hey, Mikey!

6 (VO) When you bring Life home, don't tell the kids it's one of those nutritional cereals you've been trying to get them to eat. You're the only one who has to know.

Sara Lee

"Nobody doesn't like Sara Lee."

Sara Lee had a problem it didn't think it had. And it didn't have the problem it thought it had.

Its marketing professionals felt that Sara Lee was threatened by fresh-baked cakes and breads. They wanted their advertising to prove somehow that frozen was as good as fresh. Or maybe even better than fresh.

What Sara Lee *did* have was a superb line of frozen baked goods acknowledged by everyone to be the best in the business.

People everywhere were aware of that fact. Indeed, they showed it by serving Sara Lee products only for special occasions —not exactly the kind of behavior that generates high business volume.

DDB felt that it was futile to pit frozen food against fresh when it would be far more believable (and possible) to suggest that Sara Lee products be used as an everyday event, as a little self-indulgent treat.

"Everybody doesn't like something, but nobody doesn't like Sara Lee"—innovative because of its tortured English and made even more memorable by its musical theme—showed people rewarding themselves with Sara Lee products for simply getting through the trials of the day.

The line is still being used, the tune being hummed, and the product being munched. In March 1985, Consolidated Foods, the parent company, changed its name to Sara Lee.

"You can have everybody coming in on time, everybody leaving on time, all work finished on the due date, and still have a lousy ad, and fail."

"More and more I have come to the conclusion that a principle isn't a principle until it costs you money."

Sara Lee

1 Everybody doesn't like something, but nobody doesn't like Sara Lee . . .

2 Everybody doesn't like something, but nobody doesn't like Sara Lee . . .

3 Everybody doesn't like something, but nobody doesn't like Sara Lee . . .

4 Everybody doesn't like something, but nobody doesn't like Sara Lee . . .

5 Everybody doesn't like something, but nobody doesn't like Sara Lee . . .

6 Everybody doesn't like something, but nobody doesn't like Sara Lee . . .

O. M. Scott

Selling fertilizer is not generally the sort of thing that brings hordes of creative people forth to demand the assignment.

Yet that very assignment brought forth some of DDB's strongest graphics and most interesting, straightforward copy.

The entire line of Scott's excellent products—fertilizers, weed killers, seeds—were presented with a single look, an honesty of approach, and genuine educational value.

People know and trust O. M. Scott as a result. And as a result of that result, people are willing to pay a premium price for Scott products.

It's interesting to note that once an account becomes a plum, creative people clamor to work on it. It's also interesting to remember that no account ever comes to an agency as a plum; it always takes somebody to turn it into one.

You won't get crabgrass this summer if you stop the seeds now.

your lawn for up to 2 full months.

In fact, if you spend just 30 minutes every couple of months with our straight Turf Builder, you'll have thicker grass than you ever dreamed of. A good thick turf helps keep crabgrass out.

But right now put down Turf Builder Plus Halts. It's easy work, not like mowing. Just a walk around with a spreader does it.

We sell Turf Builder Plus Halts with the plainest guarantee we know.

Here in the good earth of Marysville, Ohio, where we have our main grass research farms, we grow just about every weed you will ever see.

And the first thing you might like to know is that you don't have any crabgrass right now. What you have are seeds.

These seeds were spread by last year's crabgrass when it died with the first frost of fall.

(Almost 100,000 seeds from just one plant.) They will begin to grow in May and by August you'll have a real crabgrass blight again.

So the time to stop it is right now. And it won't take you more than 30 minutes with a spreader and some of our Turf Builder Plus Halts.®

We spent 10 years just developing and using Halts here in Marysville. This stuff not only stops the seeds from growing into crabgrass, it also won't hurt your good grass or your hedge.

And yet the best thing about it isn't just the Halts, it's the big dose of our Turf Builder.®

Turf Builder is Scotts lawn fertilizer. We make it with our special slow-release nitrogen so it will go on feeding

We'll keep crabgrass from growing in your lawn and we put that in writing.

"If for any reason you are not satisfied with results after using this product, you are entitled to get your money back. Simply send us evidence of purchase and we will mail you a refund check promptly."

(We might add that Halts stops crabgrass before it grows, not after. So use it now.) You might also like to get our quarterly, Lawn Care.® It's free and it's filled with good things to know about grass.

Just write us here in Marysville, Ohio 43040. You don't need a street address. We've been here for over 100 years.

Scotts
TURF BUILDER PLUS
Halts
crabgrass preventer plus lawn fertilizer

for established lawns

The dandelion is one of nature's prettiest villains. It's not only good to eat, there was a time when people took it as medicine.

But here in Marysville, Ohio, where we have our main grass research farms, it's just another weed.

In fact, it's a bully. It pushes the good grass out of the way and takes the food in the soil for itself. This is one weed that doesn't die every year. It's a tough perennial with roots that go down as far as 2 feet.

And that pretty yellow blossom turns into a white puffball full of seeds that the wind carries all over your lawn.

You can't stop dandelions from coming in, the way you can with crabgrass.

You have to get this pest to get rid of it. But it's easy to lick.

Leave one bit of its root and the dandelion will be back.

We'll get these dandelions out of your lawn and that's a promise.

And don't make it hard on yourself by trying to dig it out. Leave one bit of that root and back she'll come.

But just spend 30 minutes with your spreader and our *Turf Builder® Plus-2®*. Your dandelion population (and a lot of other weeds) will be on the way out in a matter of days. That's our promise.

And the *Turf Builder®* in this is our own slow-release fertilizer. It will also feed your lawn for up to 2 months.

In fact, if you also spend 30 minutes with our straight Turf Builder® – say once in July and once again in September –

your grass will be so thick there won't even be room for weeds to come in. Good thick turf helps crowd weeds out.

Your Scotts retailer can tell you all about weeds. (We've probably even had him out here to see how we do it.) But you can call us toll-free if you like: (800) 543-1415. From Ohio: (800) 762-4010, from the Dakotas and Nebraska West call: (800) 543-0091.

You might also like to get our quarterly, Lawn Care®. It's free and it's filled with good things to know about grass.

Just write us here in Marysville, Ohio. You don't need a street address. We've been here since just after the Civil War.

Anything you plant in your garden wants to grow, and if the soil's halfway decent and you give it just a little help, it will. (And your own fresh peas, beans and sweet corn will not only save you some money with every meal, they'll likely taste better, too.)

Use Scotts Vegetable Garden Fertilizer once. (Just once.) See what a crop you get.

The chief difference between getting, say, up to 10 pounds of tomatoes and only half that much is simply fertilizer.

And you don't have to make a career out of putting it down.

We've created a vegetable garden fertilizer you use just once a planting. It has enough nourishment in it to last for your entire crop.

(This is different from quick-release fertilizers that give you a burst of food right away and then run out on you. They're the ones that tell you to "apply" two or three times.)

We make our fertilizer so that it releases nitrogen gradually, enough at first to get your plants off and running, and then a little more week after week.

It's this steady feeding that helps give you all those extra tomatoes, beans and corn. And one feeding is

Up to twice the tomatoes with just one feeding.

enough unless you're in the South and have sandy soil.

You can use this fertilizer on all your vegetables and you don't have to worry about harming them. It's a slow-release fertilizer, so it won't burn. Just follow the directions on the box.

The best time to use it is when you plant your seeds or seedlings. Just spread it as evenly as possible and work it into the soil an inch or two.

We've tested this fertilizer ourselves on all sorts of vegetables so we know what it can do. And we sell it with the simplest guarantee we can think of. "If for any reason you are not satisfied with results after using this product, you are entitled to get your money back. Simply send us evidence of purchase and we will mail you a refund check promptly."

You won't have to go looking for us. We'll be right here in Marysville, Ohio.

Scott's "Flower Fireworks"

1 This is Scott's Grow Flowers Fertilizer. Sprinkle some around your flowers, wait a few weeks, and watch the fireworks:

2 More marigolds,

3 Jazzier geraniums,

4 Prettier petunias.

5 Scott's Grow Flowers Fertilizer. Put some in your flower garden and enjoy the show!

6

Why This Book Isn't on Wheels

t wasn't physically possible to include every Doyle Dane Bernbach ad and every Doyle Dane Bernbach campaign into this book. Nor was it historically possible to leave very much out.

What follows, then, represents a glimpse, a look at a small proportion of an enormous body of work that Bill had a hand in or that he sparked or that he approved or that, at the very least, he didn't turn down.

"The great mistakes are made when we feel we are beyond questioning."

SIMULATED SITUATION BASED ON ACTUAL INCIDENT.

"Dear American Tourister: My life was resting on your suitcase."

Just as Joelen Martinez of San Jose, California felt her car going over the edge, it was stopped short by one thing.

Her American Tourister suitcase that was strapped to the top.

Now, we build suitcases with rugged stainless steel frames, the strongest materials available, and locks that refuse to spring open on contact, for only one reason.

To get between people and bungling baggage handlers.

Not to get between people and sheer 1,000-foot drops.

But, miraculously, Joelen came out of it all in great shape.

So did the clothes that were inside her American Tourister suitcase.

Oh yes, the suitcase itself did sustain a small dent.

However, Joelen assured us that it was the most beautiful sight she had ever seen in her life.

Clever Fox to hold 5 adults and their luggage, yet handle as though there were only two seats and a roll bar. The Sports Sedan does exist.

Swift Fox to go 0 to 50 mph in an effortless 8.1 seconds. A 1.6-liter, 4-cylinder in-line, overhead cam engine spurs the Fox to easy acceleration.

Alert Fox to respond quickly to demands of driver. Rack-and-pinion steering and independent front suspension are bred into every Fox.

F O

Rich Fox to have two fully-reclining bucket seats, velour upholstery, and cut-pile carpeting in an interior which equals exterior for style.

Sly Fox gets 37 mpg hwy. 23 city; std. shift. (EPA Est. Actual mileage may vary based on how and where you drive, car's condition, optional equip.)

Agile Fox. The engine over the drive wheels gives it the traction to get out and away. It's highly visible at your local Porsche+Audi dealer.

Why This Book Isn't on Wheels / 157

delicious...

wasn't it?

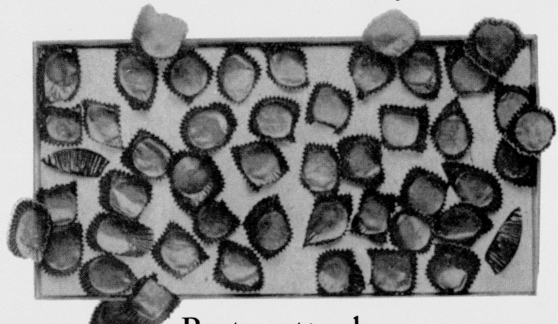

Bartonettes by

BARTON'S
bonbonniere

Wonderful Continental chocolate miniatures—80 pieces to each pound (28 different centers). See what a lot of pleasure a little chocolate can give. $1.79 a pound.

Famous for Continental Chocolates
At all Barton's 65 Continental Chocolate Shops in New York, Philadelphia, Detroit and Newark. For mail orders write: Barton's Dept. T4, 80 DeKalb Avenue, Brooklyn 1, New York.

OPEN TILL 4:20 P.M. TODAY

The story of the   cat and the canary.

(Or how to remember how real   the picture can look on color television.)

The photograph above is a dramatization of something that actually happened.

We wanted to tell you how real we think the picture is on Sylvania color television.

Of course, GTE Sylvania engineers would be happy to do so. Likewise our dealers. And set owners too.

But they could be biased. Besides, we wanted to do it in a way you'd remember.

We did. In a dramatization that's on the air now.

It's a commercial (if you haven't seen it) that starts with a cat at an open window.

He's looking into a room in which a film of a canary

is being shown on a Sylvania color set.

The cat stands there watching the film ... his head moving with the movement of the picture on the screen.

Silently he drops to the floor. Slowly, as if stalking his prey, he starts toward the set.

As the cat nears the set he stops. Snarls. And then

... springs.

We hope you'll remember this little dramatization when you're shopping for a color television set.

Especially if you want a really real-looking picture.

GTE SYLVANIA
a part of General Telephone & Electronics

"We don't do just snob ads, we don't do just short copy ads, or just long copy ads, or any particular style. If you want to know what makes DDB ads, it is a fresh and original idea that conveys the advantage of the product memorably. We have no formula."

1799-1974: Gold in an innocent America.

"Workin' the diggin's" in Alaska. For most, the riches remained the next shovelful away.

The story could hardly begin with the occasional nugget that had been encountered in the land, first by wandering Indians, later by its European settlers—it is even recorded that Thomas Jefferson found one. These were, in truth, random finds and not serious goldfield discoveries and they never committed the nation to the metal.

Nor should it start, as many Americans might assume, with the spectacular strike in California.

The real beginning took place in a pine-scented forest near Concord, North Carolina, where, on a Sunday in 1799, Conrad Reed, age 12, brought home the large yellowish rock he'd found in a nearby creek. His father, unable to identify it, set the heavy object on the porch where it served as a doorstop for three years.

Then in 1802, Farmer Reed, presumably with awakening curiosity, took the rock to a jeweler in Fayetteville who recognized the gold in it and offered to buy it.

Asking what he believed to be a large

sum—three dollars and fifty cents—John Reed sold his doorstop. It was an unfortunate transaction for the rock weighed some seventeen *pounds* and its gold value was closer to $3,600. The episode seems more comic opera than epic but it led to America's first goldfield, its first gold mine, and, of course, its first gold rush.

In a way the incident characterized a kind of innocence that has accompanied much of the ensuing American experience with gold. Indeed, to Europeans or to anyone of longer association with—and maybe appreciation for—the metal, it must have seemed that the U.S., at times, was out of synch with the rest of the world.

As early as 1803, following an upward valuation of gold in Europe, America held its price so unrealistically low compared to that of silver that Europeans could buy gold here with silver, then simply ship it home at a profit—causing the first U.S. gold drain. And the young country was once so innocent in regulating its commodity trading that one man, Jay Gould, almost succeeded in cornering its entire gold market in 1869.

Foreigners looked, too, with astonishment, at how a government could, in the absence of wartime, call in the nation's privately held gold—as the U.S. did in 1933—and were amazed that its citizens would so fully comply. Or wondered at how the women of a land so rich in gold could wear so much artificial jewelry.

And America often did seem out of step. In 1900, it became the last major country to adopt a gold standard (Britain, for example, did so in 1821; most of Europe by the 1870's) and was, in 1933, the last to leave it. Then, from the end of World War II until 1971, the U.S. alone paid out gold to repatriate its currency from foreign governments, resulting in the loss of over half of its gold reserve. For years the United States has maintained an antigold position in world monetary cir-

One of the most beautiful high relief coins ever designed, this $20 gold piece had to be replaced by a flatter version—it wouldn't stack at the bank.

cles, while clinging to the world's largest gold reserve.

Looking through history, one is able to isolate three factors that perhaps explain the American ambivalence toward gold. First, there was the nation's early preoccupation with more urgent priorities—of developing

and implementing a whole new system of government, melding diverse immigrant cultures and settling a vast land mass. Second, there was, to some degree, a psychological rejection of the metal as reminiscent of European royalties and a way of life left behind. And third, the country simply came into so much gold so fast that it may have been less appreciated in the national mind—this refers, of course, to the enormous yields which were to come from the mountains, valleys and streams of its still-unexplored West.

In the meantime, gold mining had prospered in the East—by the mid-1800's there were over 50 mines in North Carolina alone—and there had been other substantial discoveries, notably in Georgia and South Carolina. But all the gold mined so far would have filled little more than a single Yankee Clipper Ship, when in 1848, word swept the land like a brushfire: "There's gold in California."

It was the blockbuster of U.S. strikes and today names such as Sut-

Americans turned in their gold in 1933 for $20.67   an ounce. Less than a year later it was worth $35.

ter's Mill and Mother Lode, as well as many of the 49er adventures, are etched in the mind of every American, not only from childhood history books, but also from a myriad of Hollywood depictions—and sometimes distortions—which inevitably begin with a dusty false-front town or a ribald saloon with painted ladies and end with a shoot-em-up down at a corral.

What is somewhat overlooked is the sheer immensity of the California yield. In the five years before 1848, America's average yearly gold production had been 52 thousand ounces. In 1849, it leaped to some 1.9 *million* ounces and, in 1850, it was *over 2.4 million.*

Other strikes came in rapid succession: Nevada in 1849, Oregon and

The U.S. Gold Reserve Drain, 1955-1975. (Each ingot represents 2,000 tons.)

| 1955 | 1960 | 1965 | 1970 | 1975 |

Montana in 1852, Arizona and Colorado in 1858. Then Washington, Idaho, Utah, New Mexico, along with several in Alaska. Some of these discoveries were considerable but in both significance and scale none ever equalled that of California, for its strike was not only the event that opened the American West, it was also the state

that in the end contributed over *one-third* of America's native gold.

Gold is currently mined in 13 states but production has declined and America produces less than three percent of the world total. A single mine, The Homestake, at Lead (pronounced Leed), South Dakota, accounts for well over one-fourth of U.S. output. The venerable, history-rich mine, which in 1976 celebrated its 100th birthday, today gives evidence that some things have changed—there are more than 25 women working underground.

But it was also a changed America which, on December 31, 1974, regained the right to full gold ownership and one wonders if its citizens today would ever line up again to turn it all in. The affinity for gold may now be too strong. According to industry statistics, U.S. women are wearing more real gold jewelry and, at the same time, there has been considerable investment in gold—the U.S. is now the world's largest market for both bullion-type gold coins and gold futures trading.

Finally, it seems Americans are even spending time as "Weekend 49ers," poking around the old diggings in hope of finding the occasional nugget which, at the current price of gold, cannot be called an innocent endeavor.

This advertisement is part of a series produced in the interest of a wider knowledge of man's most precious metal. For more information write to: The Gold Information Center, Department P.O. Box 1269, FDR Station, New York, N.Y. 10022. © The Gold Information Center.

The Gold Information Center.

"You can get attention and really make people resent you if you do it with an unrelated gimmick. They won't like you for that."

"Skinny chickens make thin soup," says Henry Heinz. "We don't use them."

IF A CHICKEN weighs in at about 2 or 2½ pounds, it is underdeveloped and should be broiled.

It should never get into the soup kettle.

There's not enough meat between the skin and the bones to give the soup body.

There's not enough richness to the meat for a hearty chicken flavor.

A skinny chicken can't make anything but a thin soup, unless you flesh it out with gizzards and extra chicken skins and other odd parts.

And that is a cheap way to get flavor.

We like a clear, sweet chicken broth. Those extraneous parts tend to muddy the broth or give it a strongish taste. We don't like it.

We presume you don't either.

My grandfather had some strong ideas on the subject. "A customer is simply a friend you have never met," he said, "and you cannot stint a friend."

He would be very satisfied with the chickens we buy for our soups.

They are all good and plump. (We prefer chickens like Rhode Island Reds, which don't have to get old to get heavy.) Our chickens weigh at least 3 pounds. They have real meat on their bones. And both the dark meat and

the white meat are tender and sweet. This is how we like them. They are the only kind of chickens we will use. And we pay a good 3-4¢ a pound more than some other people do just to get them.

One thing more.

Will you reach for the salt and pepper when you taste our chicken broth? I don't think so. There is nothing flat about it. We add a background of spices, and the touch of good vegetables. But we balance the seasonings so carefully, watch it so closely, it is never strong or overbearing. I like to think that a man, as well as his children, can enjoy it.

HEINZ SOUPS 57 Varieties

Chicken Noodle Soup, Chicken with Rice, Chicken Vegetable, Chicken Consommé, Chicken Gumbo, Cream of Chicken, all these different soups start out with our good chicken broth. Yet, each one has an individual taste.

IF YOU ARE EVER in Pittsburgh, please come into the Heinz Soup Kitchen. I would be proud to have you watch.

"Getting a product known isn't the answer. Getting it *wanted* is the answer. Some of the best-known product names have failed."

INTRODUCING THE NEW, LARGE
AUDI 5000
AND THE EXTRAORDINARILY GIFTED
ENGINEERS WHO DESIGNED IT.

Starting clockwise at the bottom of the picture and ending in the center. They are:

Ferdinand Piëch, **Project Director:** I designed racing cars before coming to Audi. But the Audi 5000 was a bigger challenge. A racing car can be designed to last for a few races only. That is its job. A passenger car has to do much more. Besides performing well, it must last a very long time. I knew we had assembled remarkable engineering talent. But they surprised even me.

Werner Schulze, **Interior Design:** A high-performance car doesnt have to have an interior like the cockpit of a fighter plane. I felt it was important for the Audi 5000 to have a comfortable atmosphere that was not distracting, the same as a driver would find in his home. It makes him a calmer, better driver.

Dr. Anton Wimmer, **Structural Safety:** A man named Timoshenko had a theory of construction which could help make safe cars. Yet no one had ever tried it. I did try it, and the results were remarkable. I believe it will take our competitors years to utilize this theory. Someday, perhaps, this construction could save your life.

Dr. Franz Behles, **Assistant Director:** The Audi 5000 is the largest German car for the money. Yet for all its size, it is also surprisingly lively. At about $8,500,* we feel there is no other car with our combination of room, handling, acceleration, and comfort.

Jörg Bensinger, **Prototype Evaluation:** We have been testing 100 cars in the United States and Canada for months before offering the first one for sale. It was the only way we could truly know how they perform in all weather conditions here. Other imports do not do this.

Hartmut Warkusz, **Styling:** It looks the way it does because it is functional. It is aerodynamically efficient, so it requires less machinery to move it. Beauty is one thing. But if the design had not worked in the wind-tunnel, it would have been thrown out.

Joseph Eibl, **Chassis Design:** It is better to pull a car than to push it, so I insisted on front-wheel drive. You have no idea the difference this can make, especially on wet or slippery roads. When you test-drive the Audi 5000, save it for a rainy day.

Dirk Bösenberg, **Acoustics Testing:** If you have grown accustomed to noise in imported high-performance cars, you must try the Audi 5000. It gives you superb performance, yet it will surprise you with its quietness. This is why I insisted on true high fidelity equipment as an option, instead of a simple radio.

Franz Hauk, **Engine Design:** When I proposed the 5-cylinder gasoline engine, my colleagues smiled. I insisted, even though no one had ever done it before. It wasnt easy. But now, I believe we have an engine that offers outstanding performance like a 6, and great efficiency like a 4. They smile a different smile now.

Dr. Fritz Naumann, **Power Train Testing:** We designed the Audi 5000 with as few moving parts as possible to make it reliable. Parts that are not in the car can never break. It wasnt easy. Sometimes I think they call it the Audi 5000 because that's how many dinners I missed. Please come in and drive it. It was a lot of work.

*Suggested 1976 retail price $8450 POE, transp. local taxes, and dealer delivery charges, addtl.

"There will be a time when no headline is proper; there will be a time when a headline is proper. There will be a time when using a logo is the worst thing in the world you can do."

Funny that fat people have fat dogs.

"Eat, eat," said the fat master, lovingly, to his fat dog. "Have some more mashed potatoes, a little gravy, a chocolate bonbon.

"Eat to your heart's content."

Fat people generally overfeed their dogs, for the same reason that they overfeed themselves. It's psychological. To them, food means love.

Unfortunately, they may be loving ol' Blimpo right into an early grave. A spare tire around the middle does even more harm to dogs than it does to people.

So what can you do to keep him lean, alive and kicking?

Well, a fat dog is luckier than a fat man. If you're overweight you need will power to knock it off. (There's always that cornucopic refrigerator beckoning to you.) But ol' Blimpo doesn't have hands. He can't open the icebox door. Generally, he has to eat what you give him. So, steel yourself. And follow this regimen. (It's going to hurt you more than it hurts him.)

First off, get him off his gut. Walk him. A little more every day. (It might even do *you* some good.)

Then, ration your love: cut down on his food intake. Skip the "treats."

Finally—and this is most important—you've got to *get* him on and *keep* him on a *balanced diet*. (No cheating.)

That brings up the question of what *is* a balanced diet. Choose your side. Here, everybody's an expert. Some say all meat. Some swear by kibble. With others, it's chicken chow mein.

But any good vet will tell you that the only balanced diet contains a long list of nutritional components. Life might be easier for you if you knew that list is practically a carbon copy of the recipe for Rival Canned Dog Food. We combine red blooded beef, ground fresh beef bone, marrow, meat by-products and barley with healthy doses of vitamins A and D. Plus eight more essentials.

You can feed ol' Slim (formerly ol' Blimpo) nothing but Rival the rest of his days and have a healthy dog. Rival Canned Dog Food is the *total ration* idea, carried to its logical conclusion.

One last word—if you're skinny, but your dog is getting fat anyway, better check the refrigerator door. Maybe the smart son-of-a-gun has figured a way to open it all by himself.

DO THIS OR DIE.

Is this ad some kind of trick?

No. But it could have been.

And at exactly that point rests a do or die decision for American business.

We in advertising, together with our clients, have all the power and skill to trick people. Or so we think.

But we're wrong. We can't fool *any* of the people *any* of the time.

There is indeed a twelve-year-old mentality in this country; every six-year-old has one.

We are a nation of smart people.

And most smart people ignore most advertising because most advertising ignores smart people.

Instead we talk to each other.

We debate endlessly about the medium and the message. Nonsense. In advertising, the message *itself* is the message.

A blank page and a blank television screen are one and the same.

And above all, the messages we put on those pages and on those television screens must be the truth. For if we play tricks with the truth, we die.

Now. The other side of the coin.

Telling the truth about a product demands a product that's worth telling the truth *about.*

Sadly, so many products aren't.

So many products don't do anything better. Or anything different. So many don't work quite right. Or don't last. Or simply don't matter.

If we also play this trick, we also die. Because advertising only helps a bad product fail faster.

No donkey chases the carrot forever. He catches on. And quits.

That's the lesson to remember.

Unless we do, we die.

Unless we change, the tidal wave of consumer indifference will wallop into the mountain of advertising and manufacturing drivel.

That day we die.

We'll die in *our* marketplace. On *our* shelves. In *our* gleaming packages of empty promises.

Not with a bang. Not with a whimper.

But by our own skilled hands.

DOYLE DANE BERNBACH INC.

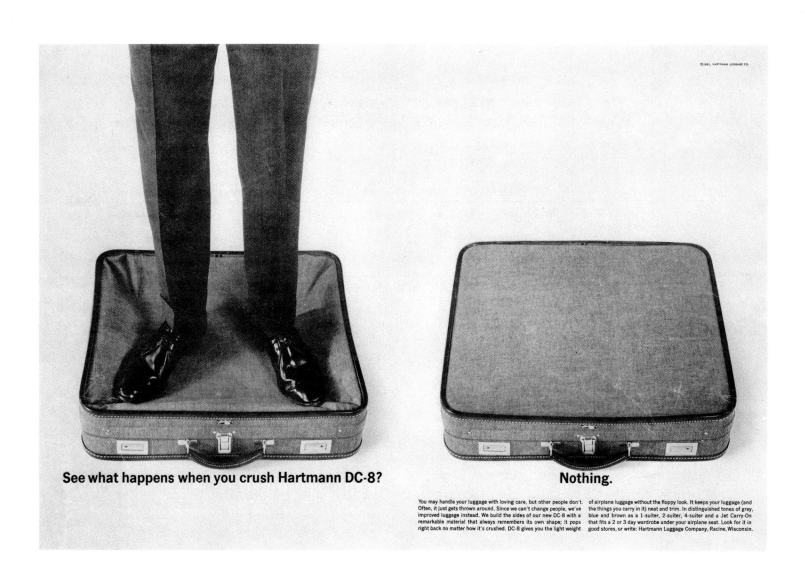

See what happens when you crush Hartmann DC-8?

Nothing.

You may handle your luggage with loving care, but other people don't. Often, it just gets thrown around. Since we can't change people, we've improved luggage instead. We build the sides of our new DC-8 with a remarkable material that always remembers its own shape; it pops right back no matter how it's crushed. DC-8 gives you the light weight of airplane luggage without the floppy look. It keeps your luggage (and the things you carry in it) neat and trim. In distinguished tones of grey, blue and brown as a 1-suiter, 2-suiter, 4-suiter and a Jet Carry-On that fits a 2 or 3 day wardrobe under your airplane seat. Look for it in good stores, or write: Hartmann Luggage Company, Racine, Wisconsin.

"Most readers come away from their reading not with a clear, precise, detailed registration of its contents on their minds, but, rather, with a vague, misty idea which was formed as much by the pace, the proportions, the music of the writings, as by the literal words themselves."

The IBM Series III Copier makes copies that are hard to tell from the original. And nobody does it easier.

At the touch of a button, it can make whatever you want: a same-size copy, a reduced-size copy (your choice: a 26% or a 35% reduction of the original), a lighter copy, a darker copy, a letter-size copy, a legal-size copy, a one-sided copy, a two-sided copy, a single copy, 40 sets of collated copies.

The IBM Series III Copier makes copies that are hard to tell from the original. And nobody does it easier.

At the touch of a button, it can make whatever you want: a same-size copy, a reduced-size copy (your choice: a 26% or a 35% reduction of the original), a lighter copy, a darker copy, a letter-size copy, a legal-size copy, a one-sided copy, a two-sided copy, a single copy, 40 sets of collated copies.

The IBM Series III Copier makes copies that are hard to tell from the original. And nobody does it easier.

At the touch of a button, it can make whatever you want: a same-size copy, a reduced-size copy (your choice: a 26% or a 35% reduction of the original), a lighter copy, a darker copy, a letter-size copy, a legal-size copy, a one-sided copy, a two-sided copy, a single copy, 40 sets of collated copies.

The IBM Series III Copier makes copies that are hard to tell from the original. And nobody does it easier.

At the touch of a button, it can make whatever you want: a same-size copy, a reduced-size copy (your choice: a 26% or a 35% reduction of the original), a lighter copy, a darker copy, a letter-size copy, a legal-size copy, a one-sided copy, a two-sided copy, a single copy, 40 sets of collated copies.

Which is the cat? Which is the copycat?

Office Products Division
714-574-5700

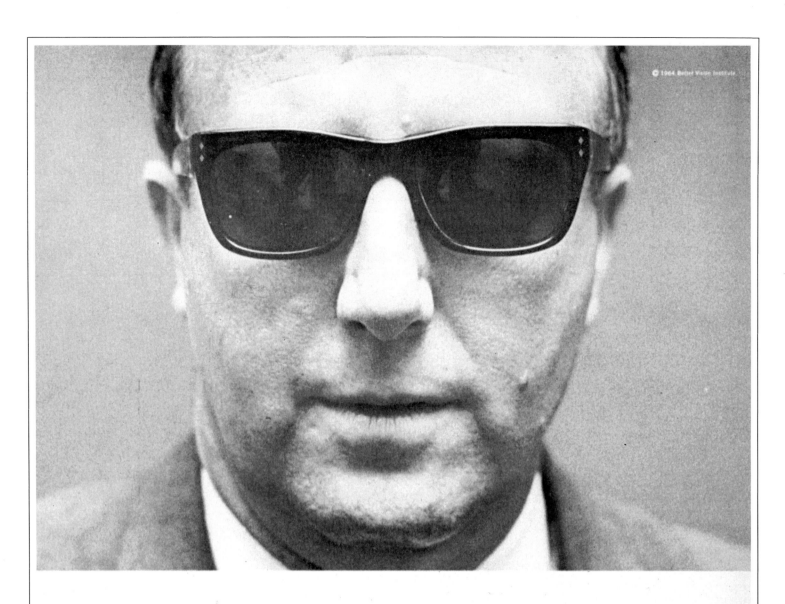

When I heard there's a campaign to get people to have their eyes examined regularly, I thought maybe I could drive this idea home by writing about it myself (with Mrs. Shearings help)

Really it should be a law, not just an idea. Seeing is one thing that shouldn't be left to chance. I know, I never had the chance.

But I have some idea of what I've missed. My career as a pianist has taken me to many countries. Judging from just the sounds and smells it must be an unbelievably exciting world to see. I'm not suggesting you'll go blind because you don't have your eyes examined. The chances are small but why take the chance? But where a person like me would be grateful to see at all, a person like you has a choice. You can assure your eyesight is all right. Or you can learn through examination that you might be seeing a lot better. I know what I'd do if I had the choice.

George Shearing

Introducing Soft Whiskey.

(The first hard liquor that's not "hard.")

Make no mistake about it, Calvert Extra is as whiskey a whiskey as any whiskey you can buy. It does anything "hard" liquor can do. But does it softer.

It's a pleasure to drink Soft Whiskey straight—there's no heat in it to detract from your enjoyment. Just warmth. The flavor is rich and full—yet it swallows easy. In mixed drinks, it doesn't fight the mixer. It blends smoothly, yet doesn't lose itself. You might call it the ideal whiskey.

Until recently, Soft Whiskey had always been a distiller's pipe dream. Attempts had been made, experimentally. But they never quite worked.

At our distillery, we tried for twelve years to produce a Soft Whiskey. About 22,000 experiments. Only one of them successful. (Anyone who tries to reproduce Soft Whiskey has his work cut out for him.)

To protect all our hard work, there are certain things about the distilling, aging and blending of Soft Whiskey that we have to keep to ourselves. One thing we *can* tell you is that in order to eliminate one cause of harshness, we have to do some of our distilling in small batches instead of giant ones. Many of the other things we do have never been done before.

Before you sample Calvert Extra, the Soft Whiskey, there's something you ought to know: you may never touch a drop of "hard" liquor again.

BLENDED WHISKEY · 86 PROOF · 65% GRAIN NEUTRAL SPIRITS · CALVERT DIST. CO., LOUISVILLE, KY.

This is an ad for a razor blade.

That's right. A razor blade.

A new razor blade from Gillette that brings shaving one step closer to the effortless.

(But what about that frying pan over there? What in the world does that have to do with a razor blade?)

Ah. We were just coming to that.

Baked onto the cutting edge of this razor blade is a miracle plastic which is closely related to the coating that's used on the non-stick frying pans.

It's known as a solid fluorocarbon polymer, and it's fantastic stuff.

On a frying pan, the scientists know why it does what it does. But when we put this coating onto the cutting edge of a razor blade, something mysterious takes place: You can slice through your beard with a fraction of the pull

you would feel if the same blade didn't have the coating.

You have to experience it to believe it.

But even Gillette, which invented this type of blade, and has a patent on it—even Gillette can't explain why it works.

This solid fluorocarbon polymer has many secrets, and it gives them up grudgingly.

After working with this substance for years, Gillette has found a way to make it behave on the edge of a razor blade. It is a microscopically thin film, extremely hard and smooth, and it stays on the blade edge to do whatever it does for shave after shave.

Try this new razor blade yourself and see if you don't notice the difference immediately.

Ask for the Gillette Super Stainless. One of the sweet mysteries of life.

"At the heart of an effective creative philosophy is the belief that nothing is so powerful as an insight into human nature, what compulsions drive a man, what instincts dominate his actions, even though his language so often camouflages what really motivates him."

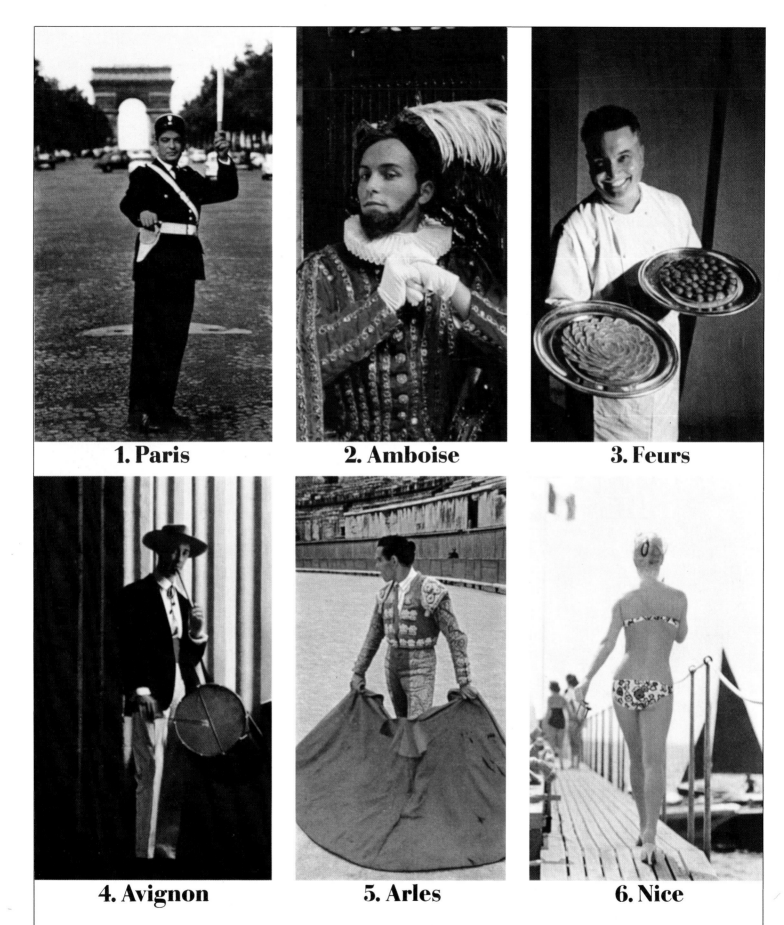

1. Paris

2. Amboise

3. Feurs

4. Avignon

5. Arles

6. Nice

Take the connoisseur's road from Paris to Nice and <u>know</u> France.

1. Beyond Paris you'll find the untrampled France that delights real travelers. Take the quiet, gentle roads through the provincial towns. **2.** Stop at Amboise where in a storybook castle you'll relive the great majesty of François I's day. **3.** Go to Feurs, a village with a great Lyonnaise restaurant, le Chapeau Rouge. Don't miss the specialty: a delicate orange pie oozing with fresh orange juice.

4. Amble on to Avignon for the famous drama festival in the Pope's Palace, a medieval masterpiece. **5.** And to Arles for the unique French bullfight in a Roman arena. **6.** From Arles it's a hop to the Riviera and the exciting coast road to Nice. Here, on the shores of the Mediterranean, you can contemplate the wonders of France, the *real* France between Paris and Nice that only a connoisseur ever sees.

See your travel agent . . . or for further information or folders write: Dept. NY-4, P.O. Box #221, New York 10, N.Y.; French Government Tourist Office: New York · Chicago · San Francisco · Los Angeles · Montreal

Sight-see your way to Europe on the Sunlane. The air is warm, you and the ocean are relaxed sailing the southern route. And, romantic ports of call beckon. On your way to Nice (isn't it lovely pictured above), see old and new Casablanca, and visit Algeciras, neighbor of Gibraltar. Palma, Naples follow and you debark for a look at Amalfi, Sorrento and, above all, Rome. Genoa ushers you into the Italian Riviera. Sound wonderful? Ask your travel agent about it, and also about Sunlane cruises to the Mediterranean. **CONSTITUTION & INDEPENDENCE** · American Export Lines

Just a reminder. We have 550 wallpaper patterns on sale now.

And that includes just about any type of design you'd like to see on this wall. All for 20% to 30% off regular price at Sherwin-Williams stores. But you'll have to hurry. Because this sale only lasts from April 25th to May 31st. After that, you could end up facing this kind of emptiness until we have our next one.

Tummy Television

The 5 inch Sony, for waist sizes 38 to 46. (For smaller tummies, buy the 4 inch set.) Our 32 non-heating, long-living transistors plus our telescopic antenna give you flicker-free reception—even if you jiggle when you laugh. The Sony works on AC wall plug or clip-on battery pack. So that your wife can sleep, we also include a personal ear plug. The beauty of a TV set this small: when you've had a bellyful of television, you hide it under the pillow.

Lightweight 5 inch SONY TV

"Daisy"

1   Little girl: 1, 2, 3, 4, 5, 7, 6, 6 . . .

2   Little girl: 8, 9, 9 . . .

3   (VO) 10, 9, 8, 7, 6, 5, 4, 3, 2, 1, 0

4   (VO) These are the stakes: to make a world in which all of God's children can live or go into the dark.

5   (VO) We must either love each other or we must die.

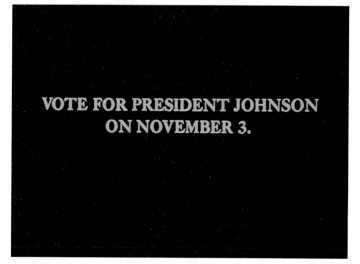

6   (VO) The stakes are too high for you to stay home.

American Tourister "Gorilla"

1   Dear clumsy bellboys . . .

2   . . . brutal cab drivers . . .

3   . . . careless doormen . . .

4   . . . ruthless porters . . .

5   . . . and all butterfingered luggage handlers all over the
world . . .

6   . . . have we got a suitcase for you.

American Tourister "Puddle"

1 Some people carry American Tourister's Verylite because it's beautiful.

2

3 Some people carry the Verylite because it's roomy.

4

5 And then there are people who carry Verylite . . . because it's very light.

6

Broxodent "200 Strokes"

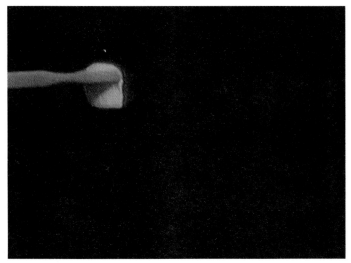

1 During the next 60 seconds, this toothbrush will brush 200 up-and-down strokes . . . about as fast as you can brush your teeth by hand.

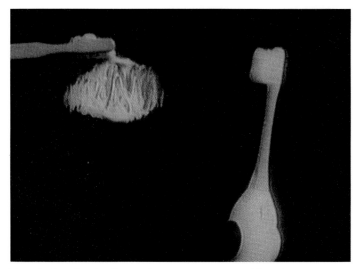

Now let's take the Broxodent automatic toothbrush.

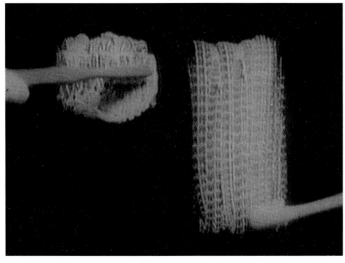

3 This is how long it takes the Broxodent to brush 200 up-and-down strokes.

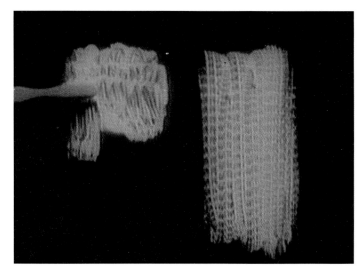

4 There . . . 200 in less than 4 seconds.

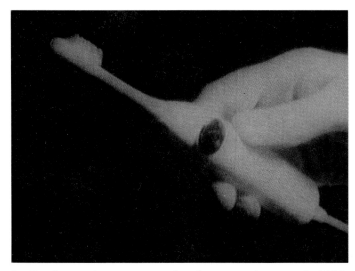

5 So, if you take a minute to brush your teeth, instead of 200 up-and-down strokes with an ordinary toothbrush, you get 3,600 with a Broxodent.

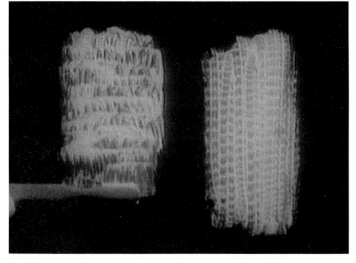

6 That just about sums it up. But we can't end this commercial till we finish doing 200 up-and-down strokes by hand, as promised.

Bulova "Clock Tower"

1

2

3

4

5   A strange feeling of certainty seems to come over Accutron owners.

6   What else can you be sure of these days?

Burlington "Sock Dance"

1 We've asked you to put on a short sock, the length most men wear, and Burlington's new mid-length sock.

2 The mid-length uses Lycra in a very special way, so it covers your shins, yet can't slip. Can't get that sloppy look.

3 You can't make it fall down.

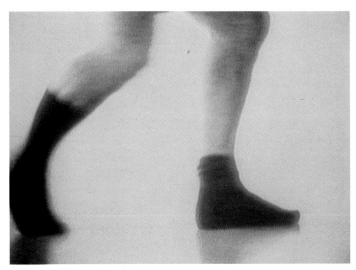

4 Nope. You can't make Burlington's new mid-length sock fall down.

5 Your shiny shins will *never* show.

6 Burlington socks. Just one part of Burlington Industries. If it's anything to do with fabric, we do it at Burlington. And we do more of it than anyone in the world.

Cracker Jack "Card Game"

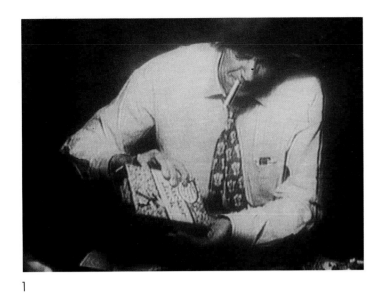

1

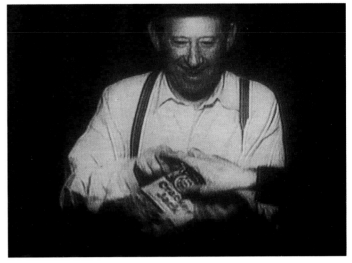

2

3

4

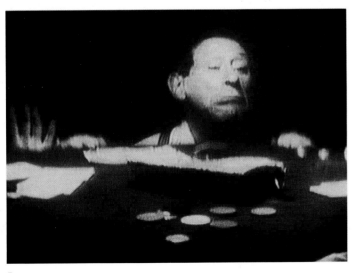

5

6   Cracker Jack. In the big Pass-Around Pack. For when the gang gets together.

1

2

3 Andy, about the race . . . I want you to have something.
Go on, open it.

4 Wow.

5 Sure, I wish you'd won yesterday. But this—this is because
I'm proud of the way you tried.

6 (VO) A Bulova can tell more than the time.

Continental "Homeowner"

1 This is the foot that kicked the skate that swung the door that hit the vase that tipped the plant . . .

2 that pushed the light that struck the picture that toppled the table that knocked the radio . . .

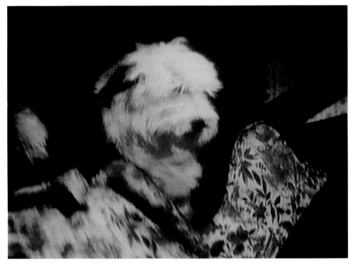

3· that scared the dog that bumped the chair that shoved the piano . . .

4 that collapsed the wall . . .

5 that belonged to the lucky guy who was insured by Continental Insurance.

6 Continental doesn't just insure the ordinary things that can happen. We can even insure the things that just can't happen. But they do.

Final Net "Dr. Hogan"

1 Paging Dr. Hogan!

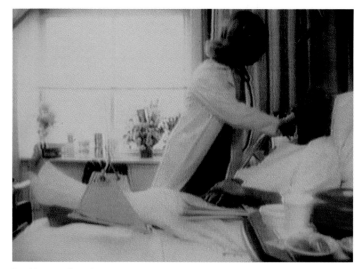

2 You're him?

3 No, thank you, dear, I'll wait for the doctor.

4 Gasp.

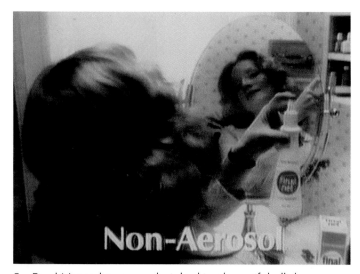

5 Final Net to keep your hair looking beautiful all day.

6 Holds up longer than you do.

Cracker Jack "Sharing"

1 I'm home.

2 Hi. I didn't hear you come in. What did you learn at school today?

3 Sharing.
Sharing . . . heh, heh.

4 Sharing?

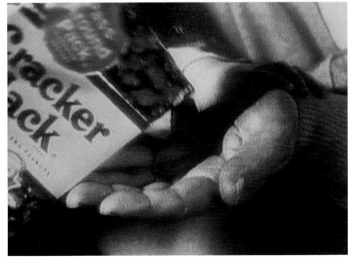

5 Sharing.

6

GTE "Burning Egg"

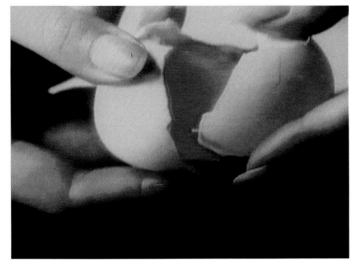

1 Cracking egg

2 Phone rings

3 Will you get that, darling? Honestly. Hello. Oh, hi, I can't talk now. What? She did? Listen, I'll call you back. She did? She didn't! So what did you say? So what did she say? She said that? Out loud? Well, what do you expect? She's just . . .

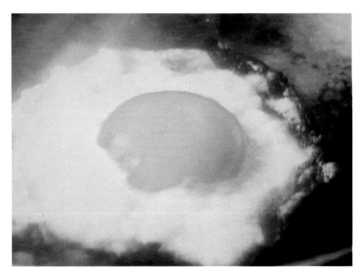

4

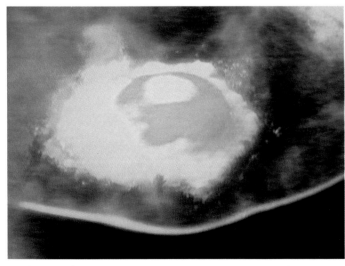

5 (VO) Why not get an extension phone in your kitchen? It costs less than an egg a day.

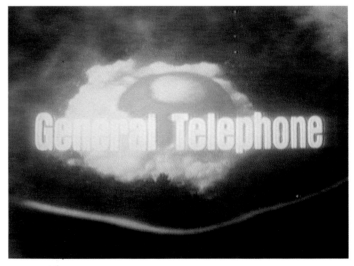

6

Sylvania "Cat and Canary"

1

2

3

4

5 You're watching a dramatization of how real we think the picture is on Sylvania color television. The question was how to tell you in a way you'd remember.

6

While he abhorred rules and regulations, recipes and formulas for creative advertising, Bill developed a set of principles or guidelines that he felt should always be honored.

As he said himself, "Principles endure, formulas don't. You must get attention to your ad. This is a principle that will always be true. *How* you get attention is an ever-changing thing. What is attractive one day may be dull the next."

Here, in his own handwriting, are some of those principles, including the one above.

SOME GUIDES FOR THE CREATIVE MAN

— William Bernbach.

"Merely to let your imagination run riot, to dream unrelated dreams, to indulge in graphic acrobatics and verbal gymnastics, is NOT being creative. The creative person has harnessed his imagination. He has disciplined it so that every thought, every idea, every line he draws, every light and shadow in every photograph he takes, makes more vivid, more believable, more persuasive the original theme or product advantage he has decided he must convey."

"The most important element for success in ad writing is is the product itself. A 'great' campaign will only make a bad product fail faster. It will get more people to try it and find out how bad it is."

"It is ironic that the very thing that is most suspect by business, that intangible thing called artistry, turns out to be the most practical tool available to it. For it is only artistry that can vie with all the shocking news events and violence in the world for the attention of the consumer."

"Principles endure, formulas don't. You must get attention to your ad. This is a principle that will always be true. HOW you get attention is a subtle, ever-changing thing. What is attractive one day may be dull the next."

"Logic and overanalysis can immobilize and sterilize an idea. It's like love — the more you analyze it the faster it disappears."

Another Bill Bernbach

Bill inhaled books and embraced great causes. Great causes embraced him in return. At the same time, his intuition about communications, persuasion, and human behavior were tested daily by the practical realities of running a vast agency network.

He tried constantly to knit together the things he felt, the things he knew, the things he learned and kept learning, into some comprehensive whole, a "field theory" of communications.

His agency gave him a forum, and he was never reluctant to take it. Once, in a ten-minute speech of introduction, he managed to include quotations from Bert Lahr, Alfred North Whitehead, Kenneth Clark, D. H. Lawrence, James Thurber, Harold Ross, Aristotle, and e.e. cummings.

His message and his outspoken delivery, together with the work his agency was doing, brought him to the attention of Lyndon B. Johnson, Hubert Humphrey, Eugene McCarthy, and Benjamin Spock, among many others. Bill and his staff put their talents to work for the people and causes they felt were worthy. Indeed, Bill often admonished creative people—and not only the ones in his own agency—to use their talent for the common good. The dedication of this book ends with this charge:

We must ally ourselves with great ideas and carry them to the public. We must practice our skills in behalf of society. We must not just believe in what we sell. We must sell what we believe in. And we must pour a vast energy into these causes.

Above all, this book is dedicated to those who will continue to energetically pursue this kind of vision, who will make the great contributions to our world of communications in the days and years ahead.

He practiced what he preached. In addition to his political advertising, Bill was chairman of the Municipal Arts Society of New York and on the board of the Salk Institute for Biological Studies, the National Book committee, and a slew of others. If you knew him, you know he didn't simply "sit on the board." When Bernbach was in the room, everyone knew it.

Bill could pounce when necessary. And he found it necessary fairly often. Here are two outstanding examples. One took place in 1962, when he took on Arnold J. Toynbee in print, and another in 1980, when he responded to Theodore H. White in a private letter.

Is it immoral to stimulate buying?

Arnold J. Toynbee, the eminent British historian who has leveled broad-scale attacks against advertising, was asked by Printers' Ink to express his views more specifically. His comments are presented here along with a response by William Bernbach, president of Doyle Dane Bernbach

TOYNBEE: Advertising is moral mis-education

"It is argued that marketing—including the kinds of new products introduced, the design of those products, and advertising—reflects public wants and tastes rather than shapes them." I have been asked whether I believe this to be true. I do not believe that. If advertising were just an echo of desires that were already in the housewife's mind, it would be a superfluous expense of time, ingenuity and money. It would be nothing more than a carbon copy of a housewife's own shopping-list. I believe that advertising does have an effect. I believe it stimulates consumption, as is suggested in the second point put to me:

"It is argued that personal consumption, stimulated by advertising, is essential for growth and full employment in an economy of abundance." If this were demonstrated to be true, it would also demonstrate, to my mind, that an economy of abundance is a spiritually unhealthy way of life, and that the sooner we reform it the better. This may sound paradoxical to modern Western ears. But if it is a paradox, it is one that has always been preached by all the great religions. In an article published in PRINTERS' INK on October 20, 1961, Mr. James Webb Young dismisses the example set by St. Francis of Assisi. "Americans today," Mr. James Webb Young writes, "see little merit in these medieval hairshirt ideas." St. Francis got his ideas from a pre-medieval teacher, Jesus. These ideas cannot be dismissed without rejecting Christianity and all the other great religions, too.

The moral that I draw is that a way of life based on personal consumption, stimulated by advertising, needs changing—and there are dozens of possible alternatives to it. For instance, we could still have full employment in the economically advanced countries if we gave up advertising and restricted our personal consumption to, say, the limits that present-day American monks and nuns voluntarily set for themselves, and if we then diverted our production to supply the elementary needs of the poverty-stricken three-quarters of the human race. Working for this obviously worthwhile purpose would bring us much greater personal satisfaction than working, under the stimulus of advertising, in order to consume goods that we do not need and do not genuinely want.

But suppose the whole human race eventually became affluent; what then? Well, I cannot think of any circumstances in which advertising would not be an evil. There are at least three bad things intrinsic to it:

▶ Advertising deliberately stimulates our desires, whereas experience, embodied in the teaching of the religions, tells us that we cannot be good or happy unless we limit our desires and keep them in check.

▶ Advertising makes statements, not in order to tell the truth, but in order to sell goods. Even when its statements are not false, truth is not their object. This is intellectually demoralizing.

▶ Advertising is an instrument of moral, as well as intellectual, mis-education. Insofar as it succeeds in influencing people's minds, it conditions them not to think for themselves and not to choose for themselves. It is intentionally hypnotic in its effect. It makes people suggestible and docile. In fact, it prepares them for submitting to a totalitarian regime.

Therefore, let us reform a way of life that cannot be lived without advertising.

BERNBACH: Only people are moral or immoral

Mr. Toynbee's real hate is not advertising. It's the economy of abundance or, as we have all come to know it, capitalism. This is perfectly all right if only he would make clear the real target he is shooting at. There are many things about capitalism that need correcting, and Mr. Toynbee would be doing the world a great service if he could persuade us to make these corrections. But he's never going to do that if he throws up smoke screens with tirades against a tool that happens to be used by big business in its efforts to sell more goods.

Advertising, like so many techniques available to man, is neither moral nor immoral. Is eloquence immoral because it persuades? Is music immoral because it awakens emotions? Is the gift of writing immoral because it can arouse people to action? No. Yet eloquence, music and writing have been used for evil purpose.

Only recently we were asked to prepare an advertisement by the National Committee for a Sane Nuclear Policy. We conceived an ad featuring Dr. Spock. Its purpose was to discourage nuclear testing. If Mr. Toynbee will agree that this is a good purpose, then he must also agree that in this case at least, advertising was not an instrument of "moral mis-education." He would also be happy to learn that here was an advertisement so persuasive that it prompted one of the chairmen of SANE to telegraph his congratulations for "by all odds the most powerful single statement I have seen over the imprint of SANE."

For the past two years we have run advertising for Volkswagen cars with the purpose of persuading Americans that simplicity, craftsmanship and low price were available to them in an automobile. These were ads that conveyed facts simply and honestly to the consumer. They seemed to sell the country on filling their automotive needs modestly and with good taste. Would Mr. Toynbee call this effort evil merely because advertising was involved? The Volkswagen was built to give the buyer the greatest value in automotive transportation. Isn't advertising performing a valuable function by making that fact clear to the buyer?

No, advertising is not moral or immoral. Only people are. I can cite many instances in commercial advertising that would prove Mr. Toynbee's point of view. I can cite just as many that would disprove it.

If Mr. Toynbee believes a materialistic society is a bad one (and I am not saying he is wrong in that belief), then he owes it to mankind to speak to the point. He owes it to mankind to speak out against such a society and not merely against one of the tools that is available to any society. He may even find that nothing will "sell" his point as effectively as advertising.

February 13, 1980

Mr. Theodore H. White
168 E. 64 Street
New York, N. Y.

Dear Teddy:

Your current article in Life is, as usual, most impressive. You make vivid the catalyst role of communications in our political life. It may be interesting, even useful for you, if I fleshed out the bare bones of your remarks concerning me.

You may remember our first luncheon together in your lovely New York brownstone. Your excitement about our Johnson commercials had prompted your inviting me. My excitement matched yours.

I did not look upon the Johnson assignment as an account. Had we not been chosen by Johnson I would certainly not have then sought the Goldwater account. I felt, rightly or wrongly, that the election of Goldwater could have been disastrous for our nation, indeed, for the world. Senator Goldwater is a good human being and is not afraid to say what he honestly feels. He is not guilty of the hypocrisy of many of his colleagues who may be his intellectual superiors but hide their real sentiments behind their political ambitions. Unfortunately, Mr. Goldwater's sincerity cannot guarantee the quality of his ideas. As a matter of fact, that sincerity can do much damage for it brings the persuasive weight of a sincere man to careless thinking.

It was this concern that led me into the 1964 campaign.

It was only later, years later, that our enthusiasm, yours and mine, waned. You may remember a discussion you and I had at a luncheon in Philip Johnson's Connecticut home to which Ada Louise Huxtable and Eli Jacobs were also witness.

It was you who opened the conversation. "Bill," you said, "you were my hero. Now I'm not sure you're not a villain."

You had come to question the use of a skill in persuasion when practiced to "sell" a man running for office. You must have entertained the terrible thought that the greater the artistry of that persuader the more effective he would be in electing the wrong man. And that the more unethically he used those skills the more damage he would do to our country.

But isn't that true about all artists be they writers, painters, musicians? Isn't it true that the greater their skill, the more they can corrupt or mislead? Aren't they the emotion builders who carry the exciting banners around which people have rallied through the ages?

I told you I had the same concerns, that I had done much thinking and had come to the conclusion that the world was going to turn on communications: that all people with skills have a compulsion to practice those skills, and that those compulsions should be directed toward worthy causes. I have seen too many good causes fail for want of expertness in communicating with the public, and too many evil ones succeed for having it; for morality doesn't come with that expertness. That comes only with the man. There is absolutely no relationship between the worthiness of an enterprise and the communications skill expended in its behalf. Men of goodwill are not necessarily good communicators. And that can be a tragedy.

It is true that "the men who understand the media map are the media masters." But you must understand that the media masters are the arithmeticians, the scientists of the persuasion process. Their contribution is more and more basic but standard, and easily available to all candidates. This is a fact that we learned a long time ago in the advertising business. You can talk to the right people, in the right places, and say the right things, and still fail miserably. Ultimately your most powerful weapon is artistry applied to a deep insight into human nature.

You said in your Life article:

"Goldwater was a man of such stark candor that he could usually be
   relied on to produce a prickly and quotable truth that would arouse
   millions and enrage more. TV murdered him."

TV didn't murder him. He murdered himself. It wasn't the prickly and quotable truth that did him in. It was his thoughtless, superficial, angry utterances. They revealed an uncontrolled personality that could, I thought, do irreparable damage to a country led by such a man:

"If I had my way I'd lob a bomb into the Kremlin."

"I would saw off the eastern seaboard of the U.S. and let it float out
   to sea."

"I would auction off the T.V.A."

He was our copywriter and spokesman in the Johnson commercials. The words were his. If he didn't mean them he shouldn't have uttered them. His remarks about the uselessness of social security cannot be excused as a horseback opinion. A more accurate estimate of those remarks would be better described by referring to another part of the horse's anatomy.

He was an angry man, and anger begets anger and triggers conflict. Should a man who begets anger be at the controls of our nation? That was why we worked with Bill Moyers in behalf of Johnson. A presidential candidate was not just another product on which to make money. It was for us at that time a burning cause on which the survival of our country depended. Were we wrong? Perhaps. But we believed.

It has been many years now since we instituted a policy not to engage in any more political advertising. Over those years we had grown to be one of the largest agencies in the world. In an organization that size you have every kind of political opinion among your people. We did not want to impose our views on our staff. As a matter fact "our" views, the management's, are no longer a single view.

So I left the political arena not because I think it's devil's work. I think it's important work.

Skillful communicators who can speak for themselves without compromising their staffs should exert their skills in behalf of men they believe in. They owe that to themselves and to the society in which they have prospered.

Sincerely,
William Bernbach

WB:as

Other People, Other Places

t is a great mistake to think that the "creative revolution" in America began in the 1960s. The advertising campaigns for Ohrbach's, Levy's, El Al, Polaroid, American Airlines, and Volkswagen were all 1950s phenomena. That those campaigns (along with many others) endured into and beyond the sixties simply confirms their greatness.

It would be closer to the truth to say that with that kind of advertising as a backdrop, the "revolution" flourished in America in the 1960s and began to be felt in the rest of the world at the same time.

It *is* true that a handful of American manufacturers, with the help of their American advertising agencies, had been establishing international markets for their American products in the fifties and sixties.

In 1962, in a pivotal conversation between Bill Bernbach and Dr. Heinz Nordhoff (the man who resurrected Volkswagen after the war), a great issue was raised: Should (or could) DDB, an American advertising agency, be in the business of advertising a German product to the German public?

"Many of my people," said Nordhoff, "are telling me that what worked in America won't work here. How do *you* feel?"

Bill answered by saying, "I think people are people, and I think the German people will react." Nordhoff agreed. "That's the way I feel too. So let's go ahead."

Bill's underlying philosophy and basic points of view were, as a Volkswagen ad once said, "as American as apple strudel."

Their universality not only allowed but *demanded* local color and local marketing factors to determine the "how-to" of advertising. (You can't run "Think Small" in a country where the VW isn't the smallest car.) The "what-to" and "why-to" aspects of advertising remained constant everywhere.

This idea, simple as it sounds, attracted thoughtful advertising people everywhere. It sparked the beginning of the creative revolution throughout Europe and subsequently throughout the world.

In my address to DDB shareholders at the thirtieth anniversary meeting, I concluded by saying, "Wherever I go in the world, when people ask me what I do, I tell them I work for an advertising agency, and they say, 'Oh.' But when I tell them that the agency I work for is Doyle Dane Bernbach, they say, 'Ah!' That little difference—between 'Oh' and 'Ah'—is what makes it all worthwhile."

This altogether remarkable feeling about DDB has created an equally remarkable kinship among its people. And the kinship has been able to maintain itself and renew itself because of the talent and the dignity of those who were attracted to begin with and those whom they attracted in their turn.

The following pages contain some outstanding examples of their work.

«Perhaps the world's finest underwear...»

"Advertising doesn't create a product advantage.
 It can only convey it."

"Be provocative. But be sure your provocativeness stems from your product. You are *not* right if in your ad you stand a man on his head *just* to get attention. You *are* right if you have him on his head to show how your product keeps things from falling out of his pockets."

"Just because your ad looks good is no insurance that it will get looked at. How many people do you know who are impeccably groomed . . . but dull?"

THE MOST RELIABLE LIGHTER IN THE WORLD.

Bryant and May   PO Box 23   Fairfield Rd   London E3 2QE

"We don't ask research to do what it was never meant
to do, and that is to get an idea."

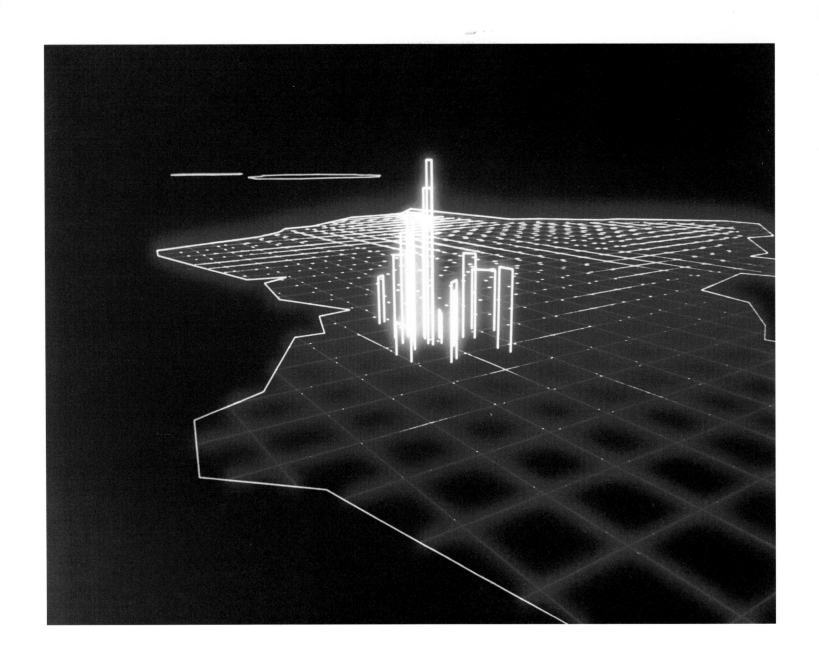

"You've got to believe in your product . . . you've got to believe in your work. Only a deep belief will generate the vitality and energy that give life to your work."

"Technique for its own sake can be disastrous. Because, after a while, you're so anxious to do things differently, and do them better and funnier and more brilliantly than the next guy, that that becomes the goal of the ad, instead of the selling of the merchandise."

A l'arrière-plan, couple de guépards dans le Parc national Amboseli, au Kenya.

Noble race

Des escarpins très à part. Admirez ce chevreau souple, ces talons allurés de 7 cm, cette forme féline et séduisante et ces garnitures bronze très mode. Le nec plus ultra de la collection Bally Madeleine. En mousse, médoc et bleu, les teintes actuelles qui donnent le ton aux accessoires.

BALLY
Le pas vers la mode

"Don't confuse good taste with the absence of taste."

"It took millions of years for man's instincts to develop.
It will take millions more for them to even vary.
It is fashionable to talk about changing man.
A communicator must be concerned with *un*changing man,
with his obsessive drive to survive, to be admired,
to succeed, to love, to take care of his own."

"In communications, familiarity breeds apathy."

Un caffè corretto con tutto il tuo amore.
Offrilo a chi, ogni mattina, ti fa trovare il caffè caldo.

In un regalo d'oro c'è sempre amore.
Ma ora c'è anche un pizzico d'intelligenza.

"Rules are what the artist breaks; the memorable never
emerged from a formula."

Bill died of leukemia on October 2, 1982.

I visited him in the hospital with Helmut Krone, one of DDB's most illustrious art directors, a short time before. The last words we heard him say were "I'll be back on Monday, and we'll do some great stuff."

In a way, that's precisely what happened.

Helmut and I were asked to prepare an obituary for Bill. The first paragraph is, of course, a quotation of his. The second paragraph is Helmut's. The third is mine.

It wasn't planned or designed to be that way; it just happened.

We did what we always did.

We made an ad together.

Bill Bernbach
1911-1982

He said,
"The real giants have always been poets,
men who jumped from facts
into the realm of imagination and ideas."

He elevated advertising to high art
and our jobs to a profession.

He made a difference.

Bill's funeral was held in the United Nations chapel in New York City. Mourners from nearly everywhere on earth came, more than the chapel could hold. Many, many of them waited respectfully outside on that mild October morning while Monsignor Eugene Clark offered a prayer and while I offered this eulogy.

Evelyn and John and Paul asked me to say what's in my heart about Bill today.

My name is Bob Levenson and I've worked for Bill Bernbach for a very long time.

Not so very long ago, Evelyn and Bill were over to dinner and I baked some apples for dessert. I remember how quickly those apples disappeared and how pleased I was. And that was after the steak which was after a lot of other steaks and hamburgers over a lot of years. And I was always pleased to see how quickly everything disappeared every time.

Not because I'm such a great cook but because I've always felt that giving someone food was really an offering of love. And for me that was very easy when it came to Bill.

The last time I saw him was when he was in the hospital. And I brought him a jar of gefilte fish. I know he understood the reason.

But I'm telling you this for a different reason. Because I think there is a parallel you should know about.

I believe that an enormous part of the reason that the advertising that we are known for is so good is because our work was delivered by so many talented people as a love offering to Bill.

I know mine was.

The best words any of us could hear were "Bill loved your ad." The worst words were "He hated it." We wanted him to eat it up. And we were thrilled when he did. And we tried harder and harder until he did.

We loved him very much and we wanted to please him very much. And we wanted to know what he thought. "What did Bill think?" was always the question. And it always will be.

So I think the obituary in the *Times* shortchanged him. Yes, he sat with us at his round table and talked to us about solving advertising problems. Yes, he wrote many a headline and many a piece of copy and came up with many a wonderful idea.

But that much could be said of more than one person.

Only one person—Bill—knew and understood the ingredients of persuasion and the power of persuasion and the uses of persuasion the way he did.

His creative philosophy isn't some how-to book on making advertising. It is a sweeping, comprehensive examination of humanity that incorporates biology and chemistry and genetics and evolution and art and literature and civilization itself. God knows he was a civilized man.

The Salk Institute, in granting him their Partner in Science award, said this about Bill:

> For his penetrating insights into the depths of human behavior, for his consistent refusal to acknowledge the distinction between art and science,
> For the simple act of giving of himself,
> And above all, *for his help in explaining us to ourselves.*

What the man did was to invent the wheel of persuasion. He could explain us to ourselves.

That invention ranks with the great inventions of all time. Because he could explain us to ourselves, he could change men's minds. And maybe, just maybe, change men themselves.

Who could or would argue that that force is less powerful than nuclear fission, knowing that the power to control nuclear fission rests in men's changeable minds?

He could explain us to ourselves and change minds and perhaps even change men themselves.

That is why Bill was so hopeful and so passionate about his work.

That is why he *willed* Doyle Dane Bernbach into being.

That is why presidents and would-be presidents of the United States wanted to know, "What does Bill think?"

That is why great schools of learning asked that he become part of them.

That is why clients trusted him and respected him and looked to him.

And that is why I worked for him for nearly a quarter of a century.

He was all that I've said to me. And a few things more.

A father. But I think every now and then I was his father too. A brother, in the sense of working with each other. But in the enduring fraternal sense as well.

A critic, in the most helpful sense. But blessed with a sense of humor too.

My proudest possession is a handwritten note from him that came attached to a couple of birthday ties. The note says, "Bob. Just to continue a long tradition of being at your throat, Bill."

Most importantly, he was my friend. We had lunch together twice or three times a week. We talked about our business and the way things were going. We swapped stories. We covered every topic under the sun. But he never failed to ask me how my kids were doing. And he never failed to tell me how his kids were doing, whether I asked him or not. Always Evelyn, the boys, the grandchildren.

I know he could have spent that time with many other people. But he didn't. I don't really know if I was his best friend. I hope so. I do know that he didn't have a better one.

I've written about Bill before. More than once or twice. And when I showed him what I had written, I was happy that he never changed a word. Now I would be even happier if he could change them all.

Goodbye, my friend.

Of the hundreds, perhaps thousands, of articles, editorials, speeches, and obituaries written about Bill, this one, I believe, is the closest, clearest, and most comprehensive.

It appeared in *Harper's* magazine in January 1983. The initials are those of Michael E. Kinsley, the editor.

William Bernbach, a director of the Harper's Magazine Foundation, probably had a greater impact on American culture than any of the distinguished writers and artists who have appeared in the pages of *Harper's* during the past 133 years. Mr. Bernbach, who died in October at the age of seventy-one, was a founder and for three decades the creative leader of Doyle Dane Bernbach, one of the great advertising firms that grew with the American economy in the years after World War II. DDB, founded in 1949 with annual billings of less than $500,000, did $1.2 billion of business last year in offices around the world. More important, DDB pioneered a new style of American advertising that became the dominant mode, but at the time was revolutionary: low-key, ironic, endearing, rather than strident and self-assertive.

Probably Bernbach's most famous campaign was for Avis Rent-a-Car in the early 1960s. That slogan has entered the language in a way any poet would envy: "We try harder. We're only Number 2." DDB's long series of ads for the Volkwagen beetle took that car's image as something cheap and ugly and turned it into reverse chic, thereby making VW the first successful import in the American automobile market. The Volkswagen series also influenced a whole generation of print ads with its stark, uncluttered, modern look.

My own personal favorite among the Bernbach classics is DDB's campaign for Levy's rye bread, begun in 1963 and built around the slogan "You don't have to be Jewish to enjoy Levy's Jewish rye bread." By making a public joke, and a good one, on the theme of ethnicity on billboards around New York City, these ads not only prefigured the boom in ethnic consciousness of the 1970s, but helped people feel comfortable with America's ethnic diversity in a way that any number of human relations commissions could not.

M.E.K.

In August 1986, Doyle Dane Bernbach merged with Needham Harper Worldwide and is now known as DDB Needham. DDB Needham's parent company is Omnican which, at this writing, is the second-largest advertising agency complex in the world.

About the Author

Bob Levenson is an internationally known and admired advertising copywriter and creative director. He has been called "the writer's writer" and "the best print copywriter ever."

Levenson's relationship with Bill Bernbach began in 1959, when Bernbach hired him at the Doyle Dane Bernbach agency. In the twenty-six years that followed, Levenson won every major award that the advertising business could offer, many of them several times. In 1972 he was elected to the prestigious Copywriter's Hall of Fame. He rose through the ranks to become chairman of Doyle Dane Bernbach International and the agency's worldwide creative director.

The business relationship between the two men grew into a firm friendship that lasted until Bernbach's death in 1982.

In 1985, Bob Levenson joined Saatchi & Saatchi Compton in New York as Vice-Chairman and Chief Creative Officer.

In this, his first book, he notes that it "is a book by one man about what another man's book might have been if either of them had ever written a book before."

Bob Levenson is married to Kathe Tanous, a locally prominent painter. They live in Manhattan and East Hampton and grow roses in both places.